Sex and the City

TV Milestones

Series Editors

Barry Keith Grant
Brock University

Jeannette Sloniowski
Brock University

TV Milestones is part of the Contemporary Approaches to Film and Television Series

A complete listing of the books in this series can be found online at *wsupress.wayne.edu*

General Editor

Barry Keith Grant
Brock University

Advisory Editors

Patricia B. Erens
School of the Art Institute of Chicago

Lucy Fischer
University of Pittsburgh

Anna McCarthy
New York University

Peter X. Feng
University of Delaware

Jeffrey Sconce
Northwestern University

Robert J. Burgoyne
Wayne State University

Tom Gunning
University of Chicago

Caren J. Deming
University of Arizona

Lisa Parks
University of California–Santa Barbara

SEX AND THE CITY

Deborah Jermyn

TV MILESTONES SERIES

Wayne State University Press   Detroit

Library of Congress Cataloging-in-Publication Data

Jermyn, Deborah, 1970–
Sex and the city / Deborah Jermyn.
p. cm. — (TV milestones series)
Includes bibliographical references and index.
ISBN 978-0-8143-3288-7 (pbk. : alk. paper)
1. Sex and the city (Television program) I. Title.
PN1992.77.S465J47 2009
791.45'7—dc22
2008032274

∞ The paper used in this publication meets the minimum requirements
of the American National Standard for Information Sciences—Permanence of Paper
for Printed Library Materials, ANSI Z39.48-1984.

All photos aside from screen captures of *Sex and the City* are by Deborah Jermyn.

**For Ma'am,
aka Nova Yolanda Matthias
(my Carrie)**

Carrie's stoop, Manhattan, April 2005.

CONTENTS

ACKNOWLEDGMENTS

Over the years during and since *Sex and the City*, many people have shared their stories and thoughts about the program with me, which has fed my passion for it and contributed to the writing of this book. There are a number of people and institutions I am particularly indebted to. First, thanks to Annie Martin at Wayne State University Press and Series Editors Jeannette Sloniowski and Barry Keith Grant, who supported the proposal for this book with such speed and enthusiasm, as well as to the anonymous readers for their encouraging and thoughtful reviews of the manuscript. I am grateful to the School of Arts at Roehampton University and the Arts and Humanities Research Council (AHRC), in the United Kingdom, who supported the research leave and visits to New York that enabled me to write and photograph this book. My particular thanks go to the anonymous peer reviewers at the AHRC who provided me with such unequivocally generous feedback. In New York, I would like to thank Ron Simon, curator, and the staff of the Museum of Television and Radio for the use of their excellent archives; David Smith, for his help at the New York Public Library;

ix

and Georgette Blau, the director of On Location Tours, for sharing her stories about the *Sex and the City* bus tour. Elements of this book have been presented at a number of conferences including the Society for Cinema and Media Studies and MEDIANZ in 2007; many thanks to the delegates and my copanelists there, particularly Cathy Fowler, for sharing such thoughtful ideas and exchanges with me.

I first wrote about *Sex and the City* in 2003 after answering a call for papers from Kim Akass and Janet McCabe. They started off as my editors, but along the way, and with Stacey Abbott, they have become coconspirators in the best GNOs this side of the pond; special thanks to them for sharing their love of Carrie and Co. and for doing so much to enrich my thinking about contemporary television. Thanks, too, to my former students at the Southampton Institute, and on my Representing Women module at Roehampton University, who have written and talked about the program with me in such interesting ways over the years. Steve Willmott introduced me to the wonderful world of laptops so that I could feel a little bit more like Carrie Bradshaw; special thanks to him for always being my technical support guy. Nova Matthias and Abigail Kearley both undertook the exhausting task of acting as my "research assistants" in New York; love and gratitude to them for sharing a Cosmo or two in between note taking and to Caroline Bainbridge for similarly sharing thoughts and diversions back in South London. Matt Wagner joined me in reflecting on many an episode, thereby proving once again that he combines all the best bits of Aidan and Big (and none of Petrovsky).

That *SATC* struck such a chord with me when it was first shown in 1998 wasn't merely because it was about a group of women drawn from broadly the same kind of demographic who had the kind of wardrobe allowance I aspired to. It was because of the authenticity of the friendships it evoked; single or otherwise, its protagonists formed a circle who dared to declare themselves each others' "significant others." For me, as for many women, I think, they gave a voice to that sentiment. Thanks finally, then, to my own urban family, who informed the writing of this book for me in so many ways.

Four Women and a City

HBO, June 6, 1998.

Following the success of Candace Bushnell's newspaper column and 1996 book of the same name, America's premier subscription-only cable channel unveiled its new Sunday night comedy-drama, *Sex and the City*. Loosely based on Bushnell's cult *New York Observer* column from the mid-1990s that had traversed the perils of modern dating, the book had edited together a selection of these articles to explore the loves and lives of a loosely connected set of Manhattan highfliers, exposing a brittle, shallow world of designer emptiness. It was soon clear that in its television incarnation this glossy milieu had been retained, while moderating the narrative tone. Much of the book's cold cynicism had been replaced with wry comedy, and while the competitive world and sharply observed machinations of New York's glamorous elite were still there, the television series focused on a complex but endearingly warm central female protagonist and her best friends: enter *New York Star* sex-columnist Carrie Bradshaw (Sarah Jessica Parker) and her gal pals: cynically minded corporate lawyer Miranda (Cynthia Nixon), art dealer and incurable romantic Charlotte

(Kristin Davis), and sexually voracious public relations boss Samantha (Kim Cattrall).

At the show's core were four accomplished, single, thirtysomething professionals living the dream in Manhattan, having made it as desirable women, with great apartments, bottomless designer wardrobes (showcasing their designer bodies), and enviable disposable incomes—though all the while having to continually negotiate the travails of dating in a city populated by "toxic bachelors." As such, and corresponding with similarly preoccupied cultural movements such as the concurrent explosion of "chick lit," *Sex and the City* was perfectly timed to tap into a zeitgeist consumed by the question of what women want. As the end of the twentieth century approached, with many of the battles of second-wave feminism regarding discrimination against women in the public sphere having allegedly been won (though in truth only superficially and only for some women), Samantha was led to remark in the pilot episode, "This is the first time in the history of Manhattan that women have had as much money and power as men." Situating this supposed new order and its concomitant dilemmas at the heart of the program, each week, over cocktails or brunch, the foursome would meet to swap stories and opinions about their relations with the opposite sex, and one of their latest encounters or observations would inevitably lead to a debate (the "chat-and-chew" scenes, as the series crew called them [Sohn 2004, 102]). This would prompt Carrie to pose and reflect on a question, forming the basis of that week's newspaper column (also entitled *Sex and the City*) and hence the theme of that episode. This quizzical perspective was initially accompanied by Carrie's intimate, direct address to the camera, a conceit dropped by the second season. But, along with the collective chat-and-chews, the subsequent "think-and-type" scenes (Sohn 2004, 103), where Carrie is pictured working at her laptop, her computer screen and voiceover posing that

"I couldn't help but wonder . . ." Carrie's contemplative "think-and-types" became one of the signature shots of *Sex and the City*.

week's dilemma ("Was Miranda right? . . . Is there a secret cold war between marrieds and singles?" [1:3]),[1] would become one of the signature shots of the program.

Crucially, I argue, it was through this continual foregrounding of a questioning stance that *Sex and the City* immediately highlighted its engagement with contemporary third-wave feminist politics. While this concept constitutes a notoriously contested arena, if, as Ashley Nelson notes, one of the markers of third-wave feminism has been to break with the "perceived dogmatism" of previous feminist agendas, to stress individuality and individualistic definitions of feminism, "with this focus on individualism, feminism becomes reduced to one issue: choice" (2004, 71). Indeed, one of the dilemmas of what has also become known as a "postfeminist" age, and one of the reasons why some critics have observed that postfeminist discourses can actually facilitate a return to prefeminist ideals, is that according to its tenets, women "can then use their 'feminist' freedom to choose to re-embrace traditional femininity" (Gill 2007, 243). Hence all of *Sex and the City*'s women are "conspicuous consumers," using their new-found economic power to embrace fashion and lifestyle shopping, and while Miranda may "choose" to work fifty-plus-hour weeks in her quest to become a partner at her law firm,[2] Charlotte chooses to leave her art gallery job after marrying in order to become the full-time wife of a society doctor, much to Miranda's chagrin ("I choose my choice!" Charlotte insists, defensively invoking the discourse of third-wave feminism when the friends argue over her decision [4:55]). It was precisely through its quartet of deliberately contrasting, diverse female "types," their never-ending analysis of their condition, and Carrie's continual return to the questions that consume them that *Sex and the City* declared its preoccupation with the politics of women's choice(s) at the start of the new millennium. Before the first season's run was over, it had become apparent that through this formula a quartet of television icons had been born, "middle-youth" women the world over had a new lens through which to debate their lives, and the boundaries governing what is permissible on popular television would never be the same again.

The TV Milestones series to which this book belongs, as its name suggests, is dedicated to examining those texts and moments in television history that we might call landmark. Clearly, however, what might be said to constitute a "milestone" in television programming could potentially traverse a number of arenas. Quite legitimately, we might measure this status through the audience figures won; the subject matter tackled; the stars, scripts, performances, and industry accolades garnered; the narrative or generic innovations instigated; or the originality of television aesthetics realized. In all these respects, *Sex and the City* has earned its right to be

At brunch (again): The women's frequent "chat-and-chew" scenes fueled the discursive framework of the show.

considered landmark. And yet a milestone suggests rather more than this. Outside of critical or commercial success, there is a sense that a television milestone should in some sense push or reimagine the boundaries of the medium; that its cultural impact or resonance should go beyond television; and that the possibilities of what television is thought capable of, of what it might do or where it might go *after* this landmark program, seem rendered somehow different, expanded, more invigorated in its wake than they were preceding it.

Again, in all these respects and for reasons this book details, *Sex and the City* (hereafter *SATC*) can rightly be called a television milestone. In particular, throughout its run, *SATC* captured the imagination and attention of modern-day women like no other television text of its time, attaining a currency that has continued beyond the show's finale in 2004. While not underestimating the numbers of men who also watched the show, for millions of female viewers *SATC* was (and remains) part of the cultural fabric of everyday life, an aspirational "brand" crystallizing a certain set of concerns and a kind of postfeminist identity that they might engage with both through and beyond television. Invoked by everything and everyone from travel agents (cf. lastminute.com's 2006 promotional pitch: "Did you ever look at those bars in *Sex and the City* and think, 'Why can't I hang out in places like that?'") to water-cooler literature (cf. Tracey Quan's controversial confessional *Diary of a Manhattan Call Girl* [2005, 107]), to best-selling, girl-power pop music (cf. Destiny's Child's homage to the show in the video for their 2005 single, "Girl"), *SATC* has, according to Jonathan Gray, entered into "cultural memory. Witness, for instance, how half of New York City, so it seems, has a *Sex and the City* ringtone" (2006). In the United Kingdom, in January 2006, *SATC* even featured as a specialist subject on the BBC's *Celebrity Mastermind*, while in the United States, next to the headline "Who Needs a Husband?" the four women famously made the cover of *Time* in August 2000. From its tangible influence on high-street fashion trends (for example, nameplate necklaces, fabric corsages, flat caps), to the rise of the Cosmopolitan as the cocktail du jour, to spin-off television documentaries, to the program's prevalence as a touchstone in "serious" media discussions about contemporary feminism, *SATC*'s cultural influence has been felt in ubiquitous and diverse ways. As Naomi Wolf remarked in the London *Times* in a feature passionately embracing the program, "*Sex and the City* is for several reasons a watershed, a series of female 'firsts' that speak directly to women's fantasies" (Wolf 2003). Wolf's point is underlined by industry research into *SATC*'s audience; when 10.5 million people in the United States tuned in for the series finale in February 2004 (a mammoth figure for a cable channel), it "topped the broadcast networks among . . . female viewers 18–34" (Anonymous 2004b).

What's also interesting about this figure, however, is that in the scheme of things, and certainly in terms of the number making up the potential U.S. television-viewing public specifically, 10 million or so people doesn't really seem very many at all. In the week beginning April 2, 2007, for example, *Desperate Housewives* (ABC, 2004–) attracted some 50 percent more viewers than the series finale of *SATC*, with just under 16 million (15.933); the number one show that week, *American Idol* (FOX, 2002–), attracted an audience of more than 26 million (26.668; Nielson Media 2007); while in 1998, *Seinfeld*'s (NBC, 1990–98) series finale attracted a phenomenal 76.3 million viewers (Carter 1998, 13).[3] It is with this in mind—this recognition that, at its peak, in the United States, *SATC* was always working within the restricted viewership of a subscription cable television show—that the program's visible reach and impact becomes all the more remarkable. Going on to achieve syndication around the world and (in edited form) on U.S. network television, throughout its run the recurrence of articles on *SATC* and its stars in the popular and broadsheet press (and in women's magazines in particular) was inescapable (Jermyn 2004). Its ubiquitous presence particularly bore testament to how the program had managed to achieve an exceptional, affectionate place as a privileged site of shared televisual experience and social interaction among its female fans, a status that this book in part explores. Furthermore, the broader media reception of the program was notable not only in terms of sheer column inches devoted to it but also with regard to the fervent and oppositional responses it incorporated. Following its premiere in 1998, *SATC* became one of the most talked about television shows in recent broadcast history, and this book also looks in part at how this media reception was constructed and circulated.

Vilified and celebrated in equal measure by broadsheet and popular press, commentators locked horns over the program's feminist credentials in a passionately divided critical reception. Was it offering perceptive and thought-provoking insights into the real challenges and life choices facing women under third-wave feminism regarding work, marriage, and motherhood? Or did it merely demean such debates, and women themselves, by hegemonically representing women as still ultimately consumed by the twin desires to shop and find Mr. Right (Roberts 2002; Coren 2003)? At the same time, the unsurpassed sexual candor precipitated by its preoccupations instigated widespread discussion about the boundaries of taste and explicitness on television. From being the first U.S. television program to use the word *cunt* (Jim Smith 2004, 2) to its weekly exploration of every sexual practice from anal sex to female ejaculation, one of *SATC*'s crucial innovations lay in its determination to push the narrative, thematic, and language boundaries hitherto observed by the medium.

Finally, the program's success raises other significant issues in the field of television studies. First, the extraordinary transformation of Sarah Jessica Parker into a contemporary fashion icon in recent years demands that we reconsider the common conceptualization of stardom as the exclusive preserve of cinema, as it is television rather than cinema that has conferred international red-carpet status on Parker (see Jermyn 2006). Furthermore the program has made celebrities, albeit on a less spectacular scale, of executive producer Darren Star and designer Patricia Field. This, combined with Sarah Jessica Parker's dual credits as star and producer; the quirky, "maverick" channel identity of HBO; and the place of novelist Candace Bushnell in discussion of the program, raises interesting issues regarding the program (and television more generally) and authorship—"whose" show is *SATC*? Finally, the award-winning critical as well as popular success of *SATC*—the first cable series to win an Emmy for Outstanding Comedy in 2001—demands that we examine the recent renaissance of the appellation "American quality television" and the program's contribution to this.

Equally, however, it is necessary to acknowledge the numerous critiques that met the program. Accused not just of belittling the preoccupations of feminism and modern women but also of constructing an address and a series of representations that colonized New York City and spoke to the interests and experiences of a privileged, wealthy, upper-middle-class white elite (see Henry 2004, 69–70), it would be remiss indeed to suggest that *SATC* was in any way universally embraced by contemporary audiences. In what follows, then, this book both celebrates and interrogates *Sex and the City* and examines the larger cultural implications of its groundbreaking success. In tracing this history, I write as both a television theorist, curious about and driven to understand what constitutes popular television, and a fan of *SATC*, who unashamedly drew hours of pleasure from its run and lamented its end. Purists might argue that my investment in the program as a fan prohibits me from being able to examine it objectively. But one might equally argue that it qualifies me to speak about it, from the "inside" as it were, with a particularly attuned sense of its cultural impact. Furthermore there has been a burgeoning trend within cultural studies for more than a decade for theorists to declare and reflect on their own fandom as part of a project both to better understand the operation of popular culture and to dismantle "the myth of the critic as a disinterested and wholly detached reporter" (Dow 1996, xiii); I situate this book within this movement.

Together, all the issues, exchanges, and events outlined here illustrate how *SATC* rose above the status of "everyday" television to become a referent that spilled over into popular culture far more broadly. In exploring this, within a book series that seeks both to scrutinize the import of key texts in the history of television and to make that history accessible within concise parameters, this volume cannot hope to be entirely exhaustive. Nevertheless, drawing on close textual analysis of selected episodes, existing critical work on the program, the testimonies of its stars and producers, and a range of intertextual evidence ranging from the Manhattan *Sex and the City* bus tour to fan guides and websites, this book examines just how the series managed to achieve its milestone status. It explores the series' characters, its careful generic balance of comedy and drama, its mix of both fantasy and realism (particularly with regard to the representation of fashion and the city), and how television has rarely dedicated such focus to the intricacies of women's friendships. In the six years that it ran, *SATC* became a kind of shorthand through which to articulate a particular cultural moment among a generation of "postfeminist" television audiences, each week condensing a whole series of contemporary preoccupations surrounding femininity, feminism, sexuality, consumerism, and women's lifestyle choices into its thirty minutes of screen time. In short, *SATC*'s striking success and cultural impact invite us not just to analyze the charms and accomplishments of its writing, design, and performances; the perfectly judged humor of its drama; or the moving authenticity of its protagonists' friendships but also to recognize the contribution and significance that television can have on public debate and life "outside the box."

Chapter 1

Making *Sex and the City*
"Authorship" and Ensemble
Television Production

Before moving on to a more detailed examination of the program itself, it will be instructive to first set the scene by detailing some of the history, contexts, and key players behind *SATC*'s germination. In doing so, *SATC* emerges as a multi-textured ensemble production where numerous influences and guiding figures played a crucial role, illustrating the difficulty of ascribing any single "author" as the progenitor of its success.

In fact, *SATC* can be placed within a narrative tradition that long precedes television. As Ashley Nelson has observed,

> Far from creating a fantasy world of frivolous femininity, a world that bears no resemblance to "real life" (as many critics contend), *Sex and the City* resurrects an historical and social type: the single woman in the city. . . . [From] Sister Carrie's shop girls to the real-life flappers, suffragists, swinging singles and welfare mothers of the next century, the single woman is a loaded figure in American history, one around which heated political and cultural

debates about women's place in society have often centred. (2004, 84)

The Sister Carrie that Nelson invokes here is, of course, the heroine of Theodore Dreiser's 1900 novel of the same name, which charts the rise of Carrie Meeber, a single young woman who moves from the Midwest to find her fortune in the big city, first in Chicago and later in New York. It is difficult not to see the parallels between this other, feted Carrie and Carrie Bradshaw, both of them flaneuses and urban magpies who devour the glamour and the lights of the city and who walk its streets in wonder and appreciation, both of them "sceptical that the domestic life, the married life, can satisfy their every need" (Nelson 2004, 84). In addition, there were significant U.S. television precursors that similarly focused on the theme of women making it in the city, chief among them *That Girl* (ABC, 1966–71), *The Mary Tyler Moore Show* (CBS, 1970–77), and *Rhoda* (CBS, 1974–78).

First and foremost, however, *SATC* was based on the successful mid-1990s *New York Observer* column and 1996 book written by New York socialite Candace Bushnell. Debuting on November 28, 1994, with a feature on "a couples-only sex club" called Le Trapeze (Bushnell 1994, 1), Bushnell's column mixed the investigative with the personal, tracing the parties, preoccupations, and sexual peccadilloes of the wealthy Manhattan social scene. Some of these tangentially autobiographical vignettes were later collected in her book, where the journalist character of Carrie gradually comes to the fore as a rather neurotic thirtysomething woman involved in a less than satisfying relationship with the well-heeled, cigar-smoking "Mr. Big." It wasn't long before Carrie was understood to be Bushnell's alter ego and Mr. Big as her one-time boyfriend and former publisher of *Vogue*, Ron Galotti. But it would be remiss to suggest that the literary origins of *SATC* can be located only in Bushnell's column.

"Before there was *Sex and the City,* there was . . .": Helen Gurley Brown and *Sex and the Single Girl*

The literary heritage of the program must be traced back to Helen Gurley Brown's 1962 "feminist" bestseller, *Sex and the Single Girl,* given its thematic debt and apparent intertextual titular allusion.[4] The 2003 Barricade Books reprint of Gurley Brown's book made this connection clear, with the byline "Before there was *Sex and the City,* there was . . ." and with an endorsement from *SATC* actress Kim Cattrall gracing the back cover. Gurley Brown's bible for modern women famously provided guidance on how to relish single life without compromising one's marriageability at a later date. Despite its contradictory presumption that marriage was still the ultimate end goal, and some questionable advice (workplace tips, for example, counsel that "if your fat little tummy should have been lopped off two years ago, lop it off" [2003, 101]), Gurley Brown's book was pivotal to the era's slow recognition of the desiring, sexually active, economically independent single woman. Like *SATC,* which was peopled with such male characters as "Mr. Pussy," "Catholic Guy," and "Friar Fuck," it happily categorized men according to definable types or caricatures; pondered the nature of flirting and the politics of sex and dating; and, arguably most important of all for its time, openly acknowledged that "nice, single girls *do* have affairs" (2003, 225). Gurley Brown went on to become editor in chief of women's style-and-sex-tips magazine *Cosmopolitan,* forming a predecessor or role model of sorts to both Bushnell and Carrie Bradshaw (an indebtedness perhaps hinted at in Carrie's fondness for Cosmopolitan cocktails). Indeed, noting Bushnell's previous freelance work for magazines such as *Mademoiselle* and *Self,* Jonathan Bignell has argued that the discourses of women's magazines are writ large on the show in three particular ways: "the trope of confession, the centrality of sexuality as the key to the expression of identity, and commodity fetishism" (2004, 164). In this respect it seems pertinent too to note the part played by Cindy Chupack, one of the most prominent writers on the show, who entered television scriptwriting via journalism, having written humorous essays about dating for women's magazines, including *Glamour* and *Allure,* for a number of years before joining *SATC*. Albeit in the context of very different moments in feminism, both *Sex and the Single Girl* and the television incarnation of *SATC* were driven by similar questions about women's choices and a spirit that encouraged women to embrace their newfound (if still problematic) opportunities.

Candace Bushnell: Sex and the City of Mirth

14

While Bushnell's work as the original written source text for the program has been widely acknowledged and has bestowed international celebrity on her, the crucial differences in temperament between her writing and the television show have, on the whole, gone rather neglected.[5] Generally, the debt to Bushnell's column was at its most pronounced in the first season, which drew more heavily on some of her narrative scenarios and vernacular (e.g., "modelizers": men who only date models) and where the bleak moments typical of the book seemed more pronounced. In the pilot episode, for example, male testimonies seem to be not merely pessimistic but bordering on misogynistic. As a case in point, consider Peter Mason's explanation of "The Mid-Thirties Power Flip," given during a series of quasi-documentary vox pops in which a succession of commentators ponder the contemporary dating scene as they go about their business in Manhattan. He explains that this is the moment at which single men end up "holding all the chips," as they become more eligible as they grow older, while women become less so. As Capote

Duncan elaborates, this is because no one wants to couple up with a woman over thirty-five whose biological clock requires her to start breeding straight away if she wants children. With its prevalence of night scenes and the rainy streets of the final shots, this episode is often, both aesthetically and thematically, a dark one. The subdued mood is underlined by the intermittent use of melancholic jazz on the soundtrack and Big's unexpectedly frank and somber insight into Carrie when, totally disarming her playfulness at the end of the episode as she explains she is a "sexual anthropologist," he tells her simply, "I get it—you've never been in love." When she asks him if he has ever been, he replies enigmatically, in what would become a signature line, "Absofuckinglutely." Furthermore, through vox pops, captions, the use of Carrie's direct address to the camera, and documentary-style filming (complete with a startling, grainy, French New Wave–style, skewed-camera, freeze-frame finish on Carrie in the pilot), the early episodes more overtly foregrounded the original spirit of Bushnell's journalistic enterprise. These devices diminished over time, however, as the television version began to cultivate a distinctively visually polished, style-conscious character and more upbeat humor of its own and, in particular, to develop the four women and their friendships at its core.

The fragmented social scene evoked by Bushnell was unfailingly cruel, superficial, and harsh, and often particularly unforgiving of women. Indeed, the preoccupations and cutting social critique found across her work would earn her comparisons with such distinguished writers and social commentators as Virginia Woolf (Wolf 2003), Jane Austen (*Daily Telegraph*, see Bushnell, back cover [1996]), and Edith Wharton (*January Magazine* 2003). Wharton's celebrated novels, including *The Age of Innocence* (1920), exposed the exacting and stifling demands of American metropolitan upper-class society in the early twentieth century. For example, in *The House of Mirth* (1905) she traced the tragic descent of heroine Lily Bart, a spirited but now fading beauty living beyond her means who cannot reconcile herself to the prospect of a loveless marriage to a wealthy man in order to cement her social position. This milieu gave Wharton ample opportunity to dissect such themes as class, privilege, materiality, gender inequity, and the business of marriage, issues that *SATC* would later return to time and again. Witness the echoes of Lily Bart, for example, in Carrie's stream of consciousness as she visits the luxurious suburban home of her married, mother-to-be friend "Jolie Barnard" (later "Laney Berlin" in her television incarnation, of whom more later): "How did it happen? How did you find someone who fell in love with you and gave you all this? She was 34 and she'd never even came close and there was a good chance she never would. And this was the kind of life she'd grown up believing she could have, simply because she wanted it. But the men you wanted didn't want it, or you; and the men who did want it were too boring" (Bushnell 1995a, 27).

Bushnell herself evidently courted the connections and comparisons between her work and Wharton's; in one column (fittingly published on the eve of Valentine's Day), having recounted the tale of an English journalist who came to New York City only to be pursued and dumped without reason or explanation by a wealthy investment banker, she announces, "Welcome to the Age of Un-Innocence. The glittering lights of Manhattan that served as the backdrops for Edith Wharton's bodice-heaving trysts are still glowing— only the stage is empty" (1995b, 17).[6] Interestingly too, given the melodramatic and visual bent to her description here, this particular column went on to make further telling intertextual filmic references, noting, "No one has breakfast at Tiffany's and no one has affairs to remember" (1995a, 17).[7] Through these allusions Bushnell potently underlined how her writing was both indebted to the cinematic, romantic heritage of New York and cynically far removed from it, an intertextuality that the television version of *SATC* would pursue further in its continual evoking of film references. Bushnell's summary provided a compact history of the "End of Love in Manhattan" that the program creators clearly found particularly compelling, as it was with this very column that the television version of *SATC* chose to open, while the story of the English journalist and the references to Wharton's "Age of Un-Innocence" and *Breakfast at Tiffany's* would form the substance of Carrie's first voiceover monologue.

Even for a cable channel like HBO, known to be more willing to take risks in its programming than the networks, the prospect of a television show retaining all "the big black truth" of Bushnell's "horrific" writing (Bret Easton Ellis, cited on back cover of Bushnell, 1996) seemed too risky a venture, too potentially alienating to audiences. In an interview, Michael Patrick King, executive producer of the show, described how the writing team recognized that to make the premise work on television they would have to adapt some of Bushnell's tone and add more humor: "[Candace's] book was brilliant. And very, very sharp like broken glass, laser smart, about who those kind of tragic women were in that time. In order to be in your living room every week, and with this cast, we saw, 'It has to be softer. And emotional. And "real-er." And they have to be clowns'" (King 2004).

Significantly, Bushnell's writing evidenced very little of the female camaraderie that would come to be so central to *SATC* on-screen. In the book, for example, Samantha is introduced during an evening at Bowery Bar with the withering observation, "Samantha Jones, the fortyish movie producer was there. Carrie's best friend. Sometimes" (Bushnell 1996, 92). Bushnell's biting column, like her subsequent books *Four Blondes* (2000) and *Trading Up* (2003), was brutally direct regarding the cutthroat world of dating that women "of a certain age" faced in New York, exposing the surface glamour and frivolity of their lifestyles as being fueled in reality by darkness, fear, and desolation. For Darren Star, the executive producer who would develop the show, this world and the terrain of Bushnell's column constituted "a great launching pad" for the series ("It was the idea that really stuck with me, the notion of a single woman who writes about sex and relationships" [Star 2001]), providing a framework that had to be adapted for television rather than a script that had to be adhered to.

This is not to say that in numerous episodes of its television incarnation *SATC* didn't confront the discomforting theme of the alleged "desperation" of thirtysomething single women. In the tragicomic "They Shoot Single People, Don't They?" (2:16), for example, following a boozy all-nighter with her pals, a hungover, cigarette-puffing, disheveled-looking Carrie is duped into posing for a *New York* magazine cover story about the sadness of single thirtysomething women. Her weary picture is eventually published next to the barbed byline "Single and Fabulous?" instead of the affirmative "Single and Fabulous!" she had expected. The substitution of the all-important exclamation point with a rogue question mark apparently prompts doubt and dread among her friends over brunch ("Somehow the question mark had leapt off my cover and onto each of them"), who temporarily scramble to embark on a series of panic-stricken, second-rate dates with men they would typically have given short shrift. Generally, however, *SATC*'s small screen protagonists did not adopt the anxious tone of the single women often seen in Bushnell's column, and the brilliantly written comedy of the television series tempered much of the book's dark style. The issues of the book were still paramount but, crucially, unlike the often humorless characters written by Bushnell, the women were able to laugh together, and at themselves, as they dealt with them. Indeed, Kathleen Rowe has argued that female laughter contains the power "to challenge the social and symbolic systems that would keep women in their place" (1995, 3). By embracing laughter, *SATC*'s women arguably reclaimed some of the power denied them by the culture of "The Mid-Thirties Power Flip," a position I explore further in chapter 2.

Darren Star and "The Channel That Transformed TV"

If *SATC* successfully reworked the dark tone of Bushnell's column for television to combine its sharp social commentary with a lighter touch, it was due to a first-rate team of writers, producers, and other personnel led by creator and executive producer of the show Darren Star. An Aaron Spelling protégé, Star had previously and most famously created and acted as executive producer on the television ensemble-cast teen-drama *Beverly Hills 90210* (FOX, 1990–2000) and its adult spin-off soap drama *Melrose Place* (FOX, 1992–99). It was on *Beverly Hills 90210* that he first worked with television uber-producer Spelling, the man behind such glossy television hits as *Hart to Hart* (ABC, 1979–84) and *Dynasty* (ABC, 1981–89). But while Star saw the potential of turning Bushnell's column into a television show, he knew its edgy subject matter would not translate well to network television, and hence he specifically sought out HBO to commission the project.

As a premium, subscription-only cable channel also responsible for other multiple award-winning and provocative shows such as *Six Feet Under* (2001–5), *The Sopranos* (1999–2007), and *Curb Your Enthusiasm* (2000–2005), HBO is neither reliant on advertisers nor bound to the implicit restrictions levied by them or the needs and standards of a mass audience as the network channels are. The vast majority of U.S. homes—about two-thirds—do not subscribe to HBO (Bradberry 2002; Neil Smith 2004). U.S. audiences must pay a fee over and above the basic cable rate to receive the channel, money that is then invested with an educated, niche audience in mind "to produce mini-series such as *The Gathering Storm* and *Band of Brothers* and a handful of expensive series" (Bradberry 2002).[8] While the bulk of the schedule at HBO is filled with repeats of films and relatively low-budget documentaries, it has nevertheless gained a reputation and channel identity associated with producing quality, cutting-edge television; taking risks with subject matter and language that the networks wouldn't entertain; letting shows with relatively low audience figures continue their run (where the networks would be compelled to take them off the air); giving their personnel a degree of creative freedom rarely heard of in network television; or, as one television commentator put it, emerging as "the channel that transformed TV" (Neil Smith 2004).

In an interview, Star described how *SATC* would have been unimaginable anywhere else and unequivocally lauded the channel for the exceptionally supportive environment it offers the development of new or "risky" material:

> Going to HBO was basically a real attempt to do a non-network show and to try to basically think outside of the box of television and not follow formula . . . it's sort of the best creative experience I think you can have in television right now . . . [I] was glad that there wasn't a typical network process at HBO where for instance, you've got to pitch a show in the fall and write it by January and then have them pick it up. . . . [With] HBO the process was, write the show in your own time frame. When it's ready go out and find a director, find the director you want, find the cast you want . . . [and] that was fantastic. (Star 2001)

SATC would become one of HBO's signature shows and one of its most celebrated and decorated success stories, winning multiple Emmy and Golden Globe awards. It became a program that, with its daring language and subject matter, its commitment to lengthy script development, and its high production values, shooting on location in New York with an extensive crew and accomplished, award-winning ensemble cast, indelibly bore all the hallmarks of a quality HBO production.

Blurring the Lines between Film and Television

It is interesting, then, how Star has described that he wanted the program to be like a *film*, not to look or sound "like a TV show" but to be indistinguishable from the movies shown on HBO, which he felt still to be "primarily at the time more of a pay-movie network." The aim was "to blur the lines between film and television" so that the viewer would feel no disjuncture between seeing a movie on HBO and watching *SATC* (Star 2001). Perhaps some of Spelling's influence could be felt in Star's aspirations here, as Spelling's famously slick prime-time serial *Dynasty* had previously taken television production values into a new realm in the 1980s, in particular extravagantly showcasing its women characters' sense of glamour, style, and fashion. Evidently HBO shared Star's desire to reimagine television fiction and his vision of a television show with a cinematic aesthetic given that, in a clear effort to distinguish itself from the perceived shortcomings of the medium, HBO's most famous marketing tagline declared, "It's not television: It's HBO."

In promoting itself as *the* channel to think "outside the box" of network television, Tom Grochowski has observed that HBO's very name—Home Box Office—"implies a paradoxical connection between TV and cinema" (2004, 154). It also extends a difficult conundrum for television studies and its conceptualization of quality, since in promoting itself as "quality" television HBO actually seeks to deny being television at all. Undeniably, HBO's investment and the production values enjoyed by *SATC* are clear on-screen and lay far beyond the grasp of the bulk of television drama. Using film rather than video, 40 percent of the show was shot on location, with an uncommonly high number of night shoots and a richly diverse soundtrack, while 250 crew members were required each week to cover everything from casting to sets to sound (Sohn 2004, 100–102). The mise-en-scène, composition, costumes, and lighting on *SATC* were frequently exquisitely designed. This is evidenced not merely by the series itself but by the *SATC* computer screensavers downloadable from the HBO website and from its wall/picture calendar merchandise, all of which form photographic testaments to the program's loving attention to aesthetic detail. Be it a shot of Carrie in a pink bejeweled basque walking the rainy streets of Paris under a flamboyantly oversized red Hotel Plaza Athénée umbrella, or the women showcasing that season's must-have accessories over cocktails in New York City's latest alluringly lit hot spot—like frames from a film and quite unlike those of most television programs—the series of stills in each are presented as art, as images worth preserving that the audience will want to display in their homes.

Furthermore, even while the "chat-and-chew" scenes dominated by the women's conversation were a central element of the show, unlike many television comedies, *SATC* was never static. Moving rapidly between locations and using moving cameras, the pace was often frenetic, with an unusually high number of scenes (thirty plus) per episode (King 2004), a mood underlined by the frequently punchy, fast-paced, screwball-style dialogue. While *SATC* is most commonly referred to as a comedy, strictly speaking it was more of a hybrid than this description allows, with a strong thread of drama running through it that became particularly pronounced by season four. This identity and its "cinematicness" were both enhanced by the crucial decision not to use a laugh track and to abandon the typical production techniques of television comedy, as Star "didn't want it to be shot in the traditional sitcom format, with a live audience, a set and four cameras. The show would be single camera (like a film) . . . with no audience and no laugh track" (Sohn 2004, 14).

Star's early ambitions lay in film rather than television; he has described how as a student he failed to get accepted in a film program at the University of Southern California but nevertheless took film classes and enthusiastically pursued moviegoing (Star 2001). It seems likely, therefore, that he particularly nurtured the rich cinematic intertextuality of the program, where filmic allusions abound, right down to the titles of the episodes (cf. "Four Women and a Funeral" [2:17] and "The Post-It Always Sticks Twice" [6:81]). Indeed, Grochowski (2004) has argued that with its reflective narrator, Upper East Side milieu, and loving photography of New York, *SATC* is deeply indebted to the films of Woody Allen, such as *Annie Hall* (1977) and *Manhattan* (1979). Generically it arguably bears just as much comparison to cinematic romantic comedy as to television sitcom. Some of its cinematic references were merely passing ones, but others, such as the girlfriends' shared love of *The Way We Were* (1973), shape moments of the show. Carrie pays homage to this film at the end of "Ex and the City" (2:30) when, re-creating the moving moment where Katie (Barbra Streisand) sees Hubbell (Robert Redford) and his new wife for the first time outside the Plaza Hotel, Carrie sees Big with Natasha at the same spot and bravely reprises Streisand's words, telling him, "Your girl is lovely, Hubbell."

Soon after the pilot, Star had brought in the writer/director of "Ex and the City," executive producer Michael Patrick King, to work on the show. If Star brought with him a history of successful serial drama and an eye for cinematic gloss to *SATC*, King sported an impressive television comedy pedigree, having worked as an Emmy-nominated writer for the highly regarded and pioneering *Murphy Brown* (CBS,

23

"Your girl is lovely, Hubbell" (Carrie [2:30]). The Plaza Hotel, where Carrie reenacts the climax of *The Way We Were*.

1988–98) and *Will and Grace* (NBC, 1998–2006).[9] Together they can perhaps be credited with having initially driven the gradual on-screen departure from the tone of Bushnell's column. Star in particular has been recognized for pushing the generic boundaries of popular television; in 2004 at the New York Museum of Television and Radio's seminar dedicated to his work, he was introduced as "one of *the* foremost producers and writers on television, known for . . . [defining and developing] many different genres" (see Star 2004). In particular, *Beverly Hills 90210* has been recognized as pivotal in the development of "grown-up" teen drama, while *Melrose Place* specifically cultivated and addressed a niche twentysomething audience some two years before *Friends* arrived on the scene (NBC, 1994–2004; Star 2004). On his role in developing *SATC* for television, Star has explained that "for me, the columns and the character of Carrie were a jumping-off point. . . . I created the other three women who, with the exception of Samantha Jones, were not present in the columns. . . . Primarily I was looking to create an adult comedy about sex and relationships from a female point of view—ultimately, characters, character-relationships and actual stories all had to be created from scratch" (Star, cited in Mercurio 2007, 21).

The first director Star would bring on board was well equipped to help materialize his vision of a television show that had the qualities of a movie and "a female point of view," as Susan Seidelman was an established film director known for her feminist-inclined oeuvre, most famously having directed *Desperately Seeking Susan* (1985). Seidelman was arguably the first in a series of respected indie woman directors working on the show, with Martha Coolidge and Alison Anders also taking directing credits in later episodes. Nevertheless, the irony that two men figured so prominently in bringing such a woman-centered program to the small screen was not missed by critics, who were quick to ponder whether Star and King's sexuality (both men are gay) was also responsible for imparting a particularly queer sensibility on the show. *SATC*'s liberal and playful approach to sexuality continually tested and questioned what constitutes heteronormativity. All the women do, eventually, declare themselves "straight." But along the way Samantha has a relationship with a woman, Maria, in season four, and the program continually made forays into such areas as cross-dressing, the etiquette of threesomes, and the nature of "gay-straight" men versus "straight-gay" men, thereby highlighting the instability and performativity of sexual and gendered identities.

Cast, Crew, and Ensemble Collaboration

To attribute this queerness or any other quality solely to the weight of Star and King would be to marginalize the contribution of the other writers and producers on the show, as to elevate their input above all else would be to misrepresent the importance of the numerous other creative influences, including HBO itself, that fed into the show's success. Unlike cinema, where film studies has long positioned (and debated) the director as the "auteur," or creative visionary at the center of the medium, auteur status within television fiction has traditionally been given to the writer or writer producer. Michael Patrick King has described this hierarchical difference between film and television, observing, "In movies, the director is God, the actors come second and the writers come fifth. In our television show, which is shot like a movie, it's the writers, then the actors and then the directors" (Sohn 2004, 37). Indeed, Robert J. Thompson has argued that one of the markers of "quality television" is that "it tends to be literary and writer-based" (1997, 15). While being admired for its aesthetic flair and often marked by physical comedy and visual gags, *SATC* was also very much a "talk show" driven by an attentively discursive framework. This was highlighted through Carrie's voiceovers and underlined by the friends' endless reflection and analysis, demonstrating how the substance of women's talk, both *within* and *about* the show, was inherently esteemed and legitimized by *SATC* (see Jermyn 2004). But, interestingly, by pointing out how *SATC* is "shot like a movie," King (perhaps inadvertently) emphasizes the problem of applying his authorial approach to television drama and stresses how debates about authorship within film studies, which suggest that filmmaking must be acknowledged as a collaborative process, are pertinent to *SATC* also.

Indeed, indicating the importance of collaboration, Star (2001) has commented, "One of the things I love about television is working with a staff," while elsewhere King has acknowledged the "inspirational *team*" of "smart and very talented" writers on the show (2004, emphasis added).

Prominent among these were Jenny Bicks and Cindy Chupack, who joined the series early on and went on to become executive producers. A number of the writers have variously described how discussion and the sharing of personal experience were continually brought to bear on the writing of the show. Chupack, for example, has related how a number of the program's dilemmas and cameo characters were based on her dating experiences as a single thirtysomething, and on HBO's *SATC* website she has observed, "I love when we brainstorm as a writing staff . . . sometimes we'll poll the actors and crew to see if we're in a fertile area" (Chupack, n.d.), suggesting that while driven by personal experience, the writing on *SATC* was informed by a significant collective impulse too.

Furthermore, as an ensemble show about friendship, one cannot underestimate the degree to which the performances of and chemistry between all the central stars were integral to the show's success. The four principal women were joined by a cast of regular and semiregular male stars over the six seasons, generally playing their (often on-again, off-again) boyfriends, most significantly Chris Noth, whose convincingly sparky relationship with Carrie/Parker was crucial to the role of Big; David Eigenberg as Steve (who Miranda eventually has a child with and marries); John Corbett as Aidan (the man Carrie almost considers marrying); Mikhail Baryshnikov as Aleksandr Petrovsky (the Russian artist boyfriend for whom she moves to Paris in the penultimate episode); and Willie Garson as Carrie's gay male confidante, Stanford.

At the same time, as the central protagonist of the quartet and proprietor of the voiceover, Sarah Jessica Parker (or SJP to use her popular moniker) in the role of Carrie was especially pivotal to the reception of the show. A successful former child actress, and the best known of the stars at the outset of the program, with an established pedigree in film (as well as television and theatre), she was pursued by Star for the role of Carrie and brought another heightened level of big-screen visibility to *SATC*, enriching its sense of "cine-matic-ness." While never quite reaching the Hollywood A-list, Parker had enjoyed starring roles in such films as *Hon-eymoon in Vegas* (1992), *Miami Rhapsody* (1995), and, in perhaps her best-received film performance, *L.A. Story* (1991). These films had also marked her as someone who could carry a romantic lead, albeit an offbeat one, a persona that clearly worked for the role of Carrie. In fact, Grochowski suggests that the ghosts of a number of Parker's previous roles seem to inform Carrie Bradshaw, including the quirky New York romantic comedy *If Lucy Fell* (1996) and particu-larly *Miami Rhapsody*, which like *SATC* featured Parker con-tinually analyzing the nature of modern relationships, along-side other stylistic nods to Woody Allen (2004, 152). Parker's authority on the show was formally recognized when in sea-son three she became a producer on the program (becoming an executive producer in season five; Jim Smith, 2004), while she quickly emerged too as its most iconic figure, with a rep-utation for skillfully working the red carpet (see Jermyn 2006).

She's in Fashion: SJP, Patricia Field, and *Sex and the City* Style

But here also one must look to the collaborative processes of television to understand Parker's conspicuous rise to A-list prominence on/via the show. The foregrounding of fashion and its transformative powers—an insistence on the inscrip-tion of identity and pleasure wrought through clothes, em-bedded in an endorsement of conspicuous consumption—became known as one of the cornerstones of the program's thematic and stylistic distinctiveness. Carrie in particular is figured as a fashion aficionado and designer-shoe fetishist, even taking to the runway for Dolce and Gabbana in "The Real Me" (4:50), inventively (if not always "successfully") mixing cutting-edge haute couture with vintage style and/or trashy accessories. Her passion for vertiginous footwear embraced them as infinitely desirable objects that, like art, are to be collected, conserved, and adored. Finding a pair of much-coveted Manolo Blahnik Mary Janes in "the Vogue accessories closet" ("A 'Vogue' Idea" [4:65]), she speaks of them in the kind of reverential tones one might expect to greet the discovery of a lost Old Master, exclaiming, "This is too much! How can this be? Oh my god! Do you know what these are? Manolo Blahnik Mary Janes! I thought these were an urban shoe myth!" As the series progressed and the personas of Carrie and SJP sometimes became blurred (Jermyn 2006), SJP emerged as one of the most celebrated fashionistas of her day, and Manolo Blahnik even named one of his shoes the "SJP."

The designer shoe as high art and commodity fetish: a single shoe held on a plinth in a 2005 window display at Manolo Blahnik's midtown Manhattan store.

It is here that the crucial part played by *SATC*'s costume designer Patricia Field, not just in terms of SJP's reinvention as fashion icon but also in terms of the program's overall aesthetic and elevation to style bible, must be recognized as another fundamental contribution to the show's identity and success. *SATC* co-opted fashion to further cultivate the fantastical edge that continually underscored the program, both narratively and aesthetically. Its dizzying array of costume changes, high-fashion statements, and designer endorsements was fueled by a larger gendered, consumerist, and romantic fantasy of an imagined single, urban woman, freed from the constraints of work, marriage, and family to spend her considerable disposable income how she pleases, on herself. Indeed, underlining this sentiment, Field has commented, "The show is not a documentary. . . . I never worry that Carrie's wardrobe doesn't make sense for a writer's income. . . . I can walk off the reality tightrope a little" (Sohn 2004, 67–69). While a number of Carrie's accessories came to be copied in affordable versions on the high street, nevertheless, rather like the abstract and airbrushed fashion pages of her style bible, *Vogue*, much of Carrie's wardrobe similarly operated at the level of fantasy; her clothes often constitute costumes that remain beyond and outside "ordinary" women for their audacity as much as for their cost. Stella Bruzzi and Pamela Church Gibson recognize how Field's authorial presence is inextricably embedded in the "look" of the program, both in terms of the way the show is styled and in the way the audience look at it, when they note that "self-conscious spectacularity is a basic component of *Sex and the City* and a fundamental tenet of Field's approach" (2004, 123). Indeed, Anna König suggests that due to the widespread media interest in Field's mastery of "kooky New York fashionability," and her styling of SJP in particular, *SATC* "at least theoretically doubled its press coverage by consistently securing column inches on the fashion pages" (2004, 135–38).

Nominated for an Oscar in 2006 for her costume design on *The Devil Wears Prada*, Field's fashion career began in 1966 with her eponymous Greenwich Village boutique, hailed in the 1980s as "a nightclub in the daytime, with artists, transvestites, students and other fringe-seekers flocking there to meet, mate and shop for wild outfits, wigs and make-up" (Hoffman 2003, B2). This was followed by her SoHo boutique Hotel Venus in 1996, replaced in 2006 by a new store on Bowery, where Field remains known for her inventive, flamboyant, and often risqué fashion vision (it is to Hotel Venus that Charlotte turns in "Frenemies" [3:46] when seeking erotic new underwear to kick-start her sex life with Trey). Hence it is Field, and not merely fashion muse SJP, who has been widely and rightfully credited with having "introduced millions to nameplate necklaces and Manolo Blahnik stilettos" (Hoffman 2003, B2). Making her quirky, directional style a quintessential characteristic of the show, Field would select "up to 50 outfits for each episode . . . [championing] a provocative, pugnacious, body-hugging sensuality" (Hoffman 2003, B2). She had previously worked with SJP as costume designer on the 1995 movie *Miami Rhapsody*; indeed, adding another layer of collaborative history to the making of *SATC*, *Miami Rhapsody* was made by David Frankel, who would also go on to direct a number of episodes of *SATC* and *The Devil Wears Prada*. Hence both Field and SJP have acknowledged their close working relationship and a history preceding *SATC*, with Field commenting, "Sarah Jessica is like a supermodel. . . . [She] is very involved in what she wears. She brings things in as ideas [and] her interest helps us do our job" (Sohn 2004, 68).

Furthermore, Field's frequently outrageous styling was arguably every bit as integral to the camp sensibility and queerness of the program as the script; consider, for example, Carrie's decision to walk Aidan's dog in microscopic shorts and five-inch stiletto mules in "All or Nothing" (3:40) or her

Hotel Venus, Patricia Field's former SoHo boutique and site of Charlotte's quest to buy erotic underwear in "Frenemies" (3:46).

kitsch Timmy Wood horse's head "Secretariat" shoulder bag in "The Agony and the 'Ex'-tacy" (4:49) (which would go on to sell out and became "the most wanted handbag in America" after appearing on the show [Lambert 2001, 15]). A good number of Carrie's ensembles were ultimately too eccentric for most tastes. As Nancy Franklin dryly observed in the *New Yorker*, "Many of Parker's outfits make her look half-dressed or incapable of dressing herself; she seems to be wearing underwear on top of her clothes" (1998, 75), while in the United Kingdom, Kathryn Flett observed that the "absurd combinations" offered as "hot tips this season" included "pink Fair Isle socks with heels, plus a sort of Andy Pandy romper suit" (2002, 14). But some of Field's easy-to-copy innovations, such as Carrie's oversized fabric corsages from season three or horseshoe necklaces in season four, became significant fashion crazes that were rapidly emulated on the high street, underscoring *SATC*'s unique place in television history as a show that instigated numerous international style trends, a feat more generally associated with the landscape of cinema and its stars.

All of this points to how *SATC* must be understood as an "ensemble piece" in more ways than one—both on-screen, in terms of its investment in the friendships and experiences of a collective of women friends, and behind the scenes, in terms of the creative collective and multiple precursors that informed it. Despite some observers' criticism that *SATC* incessantly retread the same well-worn narrative ground regarding the angst of dating and male capriciousness, it was nevertheless simultaneously a program in which internal diversity was key, with, for example, a multiplicity of changing supporting actors, locations, and particular dilemmas brought to bear in each episode. Indeed, applying a broader institutional perspective to the program, Bignell has suggested that *SATC* was demonstrative of a move in television toward a "multi-accentual address," as the discourses of the sitcom, the talk show, women's magazines, and other television genres intersected within it (2004, 166). From the different central female archetypes it constructed to the multiple modes of humor adopted, the program's richness seems indebted to the breadth of precursors, interests, and voices that fed it. In the next chapter I pursue a little more closely some of the generic history of the program, contextualizing *SATC* within a history of female-centered television comedy, while examining its uses of comedy and exploring how its mediation of a third-wave feminist zeitgeist made it one of the most debated programs in recent television history.

"You see us, Manhattan? We have it all!"

Sex and the City, Women, and Television Comedy

In order to fully grasp the contexts that informed the emergence of *SATC* and the program's inventiveness, it is necessary not only to look at the contributions of significant individuals such as Darren Star and Patricia Field who helped shape its narrative and aesthetic style but also to place it within the broader generic and representational histories of television itself. As discussed in chapter 1, *SATC* recurrently alluded to a range of literary and cinematic precursors; as I show in this chapter, the characteristic sense of intertextual awareness encompassed television too, its "self-consciousness" thereby fulfilling another of Thompson's markers of "quality television" (1997, 15). This chapter examines how *SATC*'s engagement with the contemporaneous concerns of third-wave feminism, in addition to the reception of the program, need to be understood, in part, in terms of how the show pushed back the medium's traditional boundaries, in particular with regard to genre and the representation of women and sex. *SATC* has most typically been critically positioned as a comedy, partly because of the conventions of television scheduling; its weekly thirty-minute, prime-time slot immediately signaled one of the traditions of the sitcom.

But examining this generic affiliation more closely, I want to unpick how the program resisted the conventions of television sitcom to draw instead on a diverse range of comic forms and traditions while embedding a richly dramatic thread, how it constituted a significant milestone in the history of the medium's "funny women," and how many of its attendant preoccupations proved perplexing to its critics.

What's Funny? Genre and "Dramedy"

The comic heritage of *SATC* was a diverse one, and humor in the show was drawn from a rich tapestry of comic modes. These varied from social satire to puns and wordplay to the traditions of sex farce and screwball comedy. With its attention to pithy one-liners and the pleasures of constant banter, *SATC* often seemed to mimic the fast-paced chatter that was characteristic of the classical Hollywood screwball. Reaching its heyday in the 1930s, the genre employed verbal jousting between the would-be couple as a kind of censor-friendly foreplay, in the process creating some of the period's most dynamic roles for women, in which they proved they were the match of any man through their command of language. *SATC* drew heavily on this tradition, suggesting that one of the reasons that Carrie and Big are implicitly, and despite everything, "right" for each other is because of the ease with which they talk in a "knowing" way and exchange gags. For example, consider this extract from "I Heart NY" (4:66) when Carrie learns that Big is moving to California after having bought a vineyard there.

> Carrie: You can't leave New York. You're the Chrysler Building. The Chrysler Building would be all wrong in a vineyard.
> Big: *Arrivederci,* baby.
> Carrie: But . . . why?
> Big: I'm tired of old New York.

Carrie: Well if you're tired you *take* a nap-a, you don't *move* to Napa.

Here Carrie employs grand metaphor in her first gag ("You're the Chrysler Building"), at which Big comes straight back with a punchy riposte that has old Hollywood written all over it ("*Arrivederci,* baby"). Ultimately Carrie gets the best line, her wordplay on "Napa" being indicative of the quick wit that makes language so important to her. Indeed, in season six, she can't believe that sex with new boyfriend Berger is so disappointing because their banter outside of the bedroom is so good ("Great Sexpectations" [6:76]). Equally, however, physical comedy and visual gags were central to *SATC,* and it maintained a strong sense of slapstick; moments after their aforementioned sparky dialogue, for example, Big bursts into laughter as Carrie sits on a box and collapses through it. Indeed, Parker notes of her performance as Carrie, "I trip a lot on the show. I actually trip as often as possible," while she also observes of her comic inspirations: "There are a lot of physical comedians I admire. . . . The people on *Absolutely Fabulous* are really in my head when I do my work" (cited in Sohn 2004, 22).

Of course comedy, whatever its specific form, is often underwritten by pathos. While generally adopting a more uplifting tone than Bushnell's book, from the very start *SATC* pursued a richly dramatic thread, tackling serious issues and developing complex narrative arcs over its six seasons that were often somber in tone and that made it affecting in ways that its "comedy" moniker often belied. Indeed, reflecting on how traditional definitions of television formats and genres are increasingly under negotiation in contemporary television, Glen Creeber has situated *SATC* within "a new subgenre, one that incorporates and combines important elements of soap-opera, drama, comedy and comedy drama" and that he designates "soap drama" (2004, 115) or "dramedy"

(142). Specifically, he notes of *SATC*'s dramedy format that it "cleverly combined elements of soap opera with the series, serial and situation comedy to produce a form of 'soap drama' that allowed different narrative levels to take place simultaneously" (142). In this sense, *SATC* is cleverly mirrored by *Jules and Mimi*, the show within the show that Miranda becomes fanatical about, as in another layer of self-conscious intertextuality she follows the machinations of this fictional British dramedy on her TiVo with the same devotion that the fan audience at home watches *SATC*. Chief among *SATC*'s dramatic narrative arcs was the on-again, off-again love affair between Big and Carrie. While, as seen earlier, this was often written as lighthearted and flirtatious in tone, in dramedy style the program would also intermittently startle the audience with painful revelations about how damaging Big's emotional detachment from Carrie was to her. In "Twenty-Something Girls vs. Thirty-Something Women" (2:29), for example, at a party in the Hamptons Carrie bumps into Big with his new girlfriend, Natasha, for the first time. She runs down to the beach to escape him followed by Miranda, but no witty dialogue follows, no clever trade of quips about Big ensues. Instead, as Miranda holds back her hair, Carrie begins to vomit, while behind her, in a beautifully shot juxtaposition of celebration with heartbreak, fireworks light up the night sky.

On occasion, too, the program would take up a slightly edifying (though not didactic) position on a "serious" subject, relating in some instances to women's sexual health.[10] For example, Miranda is seen to responsibly, if awkwardly, phone all her previous sexual partners to inform them she has chlamydia after learning both that she has contracted the STD and that it can go unnoticed as asymptomatic (3:36); Charlotte is persuaded not to fear her own genitalia but to empower herself and know her own body by using a mirror to explore them (4:50); Carrie and Miranda express surprise that Samantha has never had an HIV test and encourage her to do so, having been tested themselves (3:41). Later, in season four, the question of whether Miranda should have an abortion when she unexpectedly gets pregnant is dealt with without judgment or sensationalism, as is the fact that both Samantha and Carrie admit to having had abortions of their own, even while this storyline sits in fraught contrast with Charlotte's struggle to conceive with Trey. In an era when American abortion legislation is undergoing increasingly restrictive scrutiny, the significance of a U.S. television show being willing and able to explore this topic in such a reflective and even-handed manner should not be underestimated. Furthermore, according to Thompson's framework again, this willingness to tackle controversial subjects, within a "liberal humanist" bent, is another marker of "quality" television status (1997, 15).

Humor accompanies many of these storylines—hence it might be argued at one level that making light of these topics to some extent immobilizes a more in-depth analysis of them and renders them more palatable to the viewer. But, if anything, *SATC*'s dramatic aspects have tended to go neglected in critical and popular accounts of the show, due to the overwhelming attention paid to its more immediately "newsworthy" or arresting qualities such as its penchants for high fashion and explicit language. The perfectly observed and wholly unanticipated death of Miranda's mother in season four arguably constituted a kind of transitional moment in the program in this respect (4:56), movingly showing how it could integrate tragedy into its comic terrain and, indeed, how its actresses could deliver poignancy just as adroitly as one-liners. Later storylines would also include Charlotte's infertility and Samantha's breast cancer, narratives that were fundamental to the complexity of *SATC*'s representation of its women protagonists and their friendships and, indeed, to the passionate investment that the show's fans made in the program.

Significantly too within this, the women embraced one another as family. While a traditional family-style dynamic forms another cornerstone of the conventional television sitcom and recurrently shapes the way it models its relationships (a structure adhered to by the genre both within and beyond its domestic settings), in *SATC* "family" is reimagined in the unusually richly textured relationships that develop between Carrie and her friends as the series progresses. Indeed, it is arguably here, in the carefully observed and interweaving nuances of each character and their shared histories of both good and bad times, that *SATC* constituted an intricate dramedy, distinguishing it from other similarly themed but more predominantly comic fare such as *Friends* or *Seinfeld*. Both Darren Star and Michael Patrick King have described how, after regretting their decision to feature Charlotte's brother in an early episode (2:27), they deliberately chose not to give the women any real sense of familial background or personal history outside of each other (e.g., Sohn 2004, 55). Hence we never learn how the friends met, just as we only very sporadically glimpse fragments of their family histories (e.g., when in a rare pre–New York anecdote, Carrie reveals that her father left her and her mother when she was five [4:65]). At Miranda's mother's funeral, it is Carrie, and not Miranda's blood siblings, who hurries to Miranda's side so that she won't have to walk alone behind her mother's coffin.

The women regularly provide physical comfort to one another and are constantly tactile together, stroking each other, holding hands, hugging. Even at Charlotte's and Miranda's weddings, their birth families remain in the background as faceless, anonymous figures, ensuring that the focus always remains on the women's bonds with one another and endowing their relationships with a level of both intimacy and intensity (like members of a birth family, the women also argue fiercely on occasion) that television has rarely detailed in its explorations of female friendships. Audience research among female fans of the program found that the perceived authenticity of the women's relationships was embraced by these viewers as one of its most pleasurable aspects (Jermyn 2004). Yet it might also be argued that the program's vision of female friendship is embedded also in the discourses of fantasy that run through it, as it imagines a world where women have both the availability and means to spend so much time together, supporting one another emotionally in the everyday as well as sharing an endless stream of glamorous cocktail parties. It is worth noting also, though, that Carrie—narrator, chief protagonist, and best friend to all—is not idealized despite her central role in the women's relationships. On the contrary, even while warm and loving, she is shown to be flawed in a very human way, with a capacity for self-centeredness and deceit. For example, her destructive affair with Big in season three, shortly after she has begun dating the infinitely likeable Aidan and Big has married Natasha, tests the support of both her friends and the audience. Ultimately, however, it was arguably the writers' willingness to make Carrie imperfect that also made her so engaging.

Sex and the City's TV Sisters

While *SATC* deliberately sought to extend or reimagine the generic and aesthetic boundaries of the medium through, for example, investing in a highly cinematic look and losing the sitcom's traditional laugh track, it must nevertheless be recognized as having belonged to a genealogy of woman-centered television comedy shows. Ever since Lucille Ball drove the unprecedented success of *I Love Lucy* (CBS, 1951–57) there has been an intriguing relationship between women and television comedy, and this early show is credited with both having established the basic tenets of the television sitcom format and, within this, having entrenched the genre's preoccupations (and its representation of women in particular) regarding the domestic and familial. The show centered on Lucy and Ricky Ricardo, a married New York couple who every week would squabble over and eventually resolve a problem of some kind, more often than not focused on madcap, frustrated housewife Lucy's wish to escape the home and join her band-leader husband on the stage. With its thirty-minute episodic format, live studio audience, and three-camera setup, in Brett Mills's words, *I Love Lucy* "inaugurated the format, shooting style, social location, performance style, narrative structure and prevailing ideology of American sitcom" (2007, 105). It has been widely read as playing out the tensions of 1950s America's struggle to position women in the domestic sphere, with critical debate focusing on the extent to which it articulated resistance to, or endorsement of, the era's patriarchal culture. By the late 1960s, this social struggle was gaining momentum, and it was at this time that two of the most important precursors of *SATC* emerged, both of them endeavoring to take their women protagonists more concertedly out of the home, namely *That Girl* (1966–71) and *The Mary Tyler Moore Show* (hereafter *The MTM Show*; 1970–77).

Of the two, *The MTM Show* has been far more widely credited with having constituted a landmark moment in the representation of women on television. For example, Bonnie Dow's excellent *Prime-Time Feminism* (1996), which examines the relationship between television and the women's movement, in part commences its analysis from 1970 because this is the year in which *The MTM Show* debuted. And yet *The MTM Show* arguably took up a trajectory driven by *That Girl*, in that both shows centered on the adventures of working women living alone in the city. The heroine of *That Girl*, Ann Marie (Marlo Thomas), is a jobbing young actress living in New York, albeit never far from the watchful eyes of her boyfriend/fiancé and father.[11] With these male figures featuring so prominently in and arguably delimiting Ann Marie's "independence," *That Girl* has, perhaps neglectfully, never received anything like the same degree of critical attention from feminist television theorists as the later workplace comedy *The MTM Show*. In contrast, the latter's heroine, Mary Richards (Mary Tyler Moore), was older (in her thirties), single (and arguably by choice—in the first episode she declines to get back with her former boyfriend), and more fully immersed in the world of work (in the first episode she also starts a new job as an associate producer of WJM, a local Minneapolis television station where much of the show is set).

SATC signaled its indebtedness to these programs through its opening sequence (as Darren Star has acknowledged [Sohn 2004, 36]), as both these shows similarly opened with montage sequences featuring their female protagonists animatedly walking through the city space (which in the case of *That Girl* was, like *SATC*, Manhattan). Indeed, rather bypassing acknowledgment of the debt it owed to *That Girl*, the credit sequence of *The MTM Show* has come to enjoy a privileged place in U.S. pop-culture history. It has been celebrated particularly for the climactic moment right at the end where Mary is seen delightedly spinning round on the street as everything and everyone around her blurs, freeze-framing her as she giddily and triumphantly throws her beret up into the sky, thus capturing a momentary sense of the pleasure the city might hold for women. Its New York–based spin off, *Rhoda*, starring Valerie Harper as Mary's acerbic, single gal pal who left Minneapolis to return to her home city in her own show, parodied the sequence in its own end credits by showing Rhoda clumsily dropping her hat on the ground. In contrast, too, to Mary's upbeat finish, after a montage of shots showing her smiling among the landmarks of Manhattan's architecture, Carrie ends the credits of *SATC* getting splashed by a bus (a sequence I return to in the next chapter in my discussion of the city in *SATC*). But the intertextual reference was clear; as Nancy Franklin put it in the *New Yorker*, "It's as if Mary Tyler Moore, while throwing her beret in the air, had got splattered with bird droppings" (1998, 75). Furthermore, in "Shortcomings" (2:27), *SATC* pays a kind of homage to *Rhoda*, and positions itself within the family tree of women's television comedy as something of a daughter to that show's second-wave feminist moment, by featuring a cameo by Valerie Harper. Appearing as Wallace, the vibrant mother of Carrie's latest boyfriend and a celebrated feminist documentary filmmaker with whom Carrie instantly bonds despite wanting to dump her son, Carrie is impressed and smitten by her zest for life, admitting in voiceover, "I was in love with her."

At one level, then, *SATC* can be positioned within an established thematic television tradition, that of the "woman making it in the city." But, crucially, it was also a show that centered on an ensemble of close-knit female friends. While both *The MTM Show* and *Rhoda* featured significant female-focused relationships, in the case of *The MTM Show* this was mitigated by the centrality of the male cast Mary worked with and cared for at WJM and by the primacy of family ties in *Rhoda*, in which the heroine continually struggled to assert her independence from an overbearing mother. In terms of turning the spotlight on an ensemble of female friends and away from an individual woman, as suggested by these earlier shows' eponymous titles, it is *The Golden Girls* (NBC, 1985–92) that can be said to constitute a more obvious antecedent to *SATC* and that, I would argue, is its most significant precursor.[12]

Set in Miami, the show centered on the friendships and exploits of four older women, all of them divorced or widowed and sharing a home together. As such, like *SATC*, it imagined a bold milieu for television where the relationships between a set of women are the primary focus, forming a surrogate family unit where men play a generally peripheral role. Beyond this, too, the specific character dynamics between the women in many ways pre-empted those of *SATC*. As Jennifer Griffin and Kera Bolonik observed in the *New York Times*, "The parallels between the two shows are uncanny" (2003, 29), with each of the *Golden Girls* characters' finding her match in the later show; naïve, sweet-natured Rose (Betty White) becomes Charlotte; decadent Southern belle Blanche (Rue McClanahan) becomes Samantha; straight-talking Sophia (Estelle Getty) becomes Miranda; and measured Dorothy (Bea Arthur) becomes Carrie. Furthermore, as Griffin and Bolonik also noted, "Both shows strike a chord among young women and gay men, and the reason is their identical messages: husbands and boyfriends will come and go (and come and come again in Samantha and Blanche's cases), but the bonds of friendship are impenetrable" (2003, 29). Anticipating the intimacy of Carrie and Co. by more than a decade, in its first episode Blanche retreats from her friends, heartbroken, when her fiancé is exposed as a bigamist, until one morning she reappears, evidently her old self again, and tells them happily that she'd found herself humming in the shower earlier. She explains, "And humming means I'm feeling good. And then I realized. I was feeling good because of you. You made the difference. You're my family. And you make me happy to be alive."

The Golden Girls has most typically been understood as syrupy American sitcom fare, with scenes such as these read as evidence of an excessive sentimentality. And yet exchanges like this, which both undermine traditional family and the primacy of the heterosexual couple to privilege and celebrate the homosocial world of women, are all too infrequent on television.

Sex and the City's "Unruly Women"

The Golden Girls should also be credited with having addressed another female taboo, which *SATC* similarly tackled, namely the active sexuality of "older" women. Undermining a culture that perennially renders them invisible, the series showed instead that postmenopausal women can be both desired and desiring. *The Golden Girls'* Blanche, while of course quite significantly older than Samantha, seems nevertheless to have formed a kind of model for her, similarly refusing to give up her sexual identity because of her advancing years in defiance of the conflicts this poses for dominant culture. In fact, both of these figures arguably constitute what Kathleen Rowe has termed "unruly women" (1995). Like Lucy Ricardo before them, with her frequently histrionic attempts to leave domesticity for a more glamorous life on stage, or Sophia's recurrently shocking and improper frankness in *The Golden Girls*, Blanche and Samantha's assertive sexuality marked them both as "unruly." Whether through her "excessive" corporeality or her unmanageable desires or behavior, the unruly woman transgresses proper feminine propriety. In essence she is, in Rowe's words, "woman as rule-breaker, joke-maker and public, bodily spectacle" (1995, 12).

Rowe traces a long historical tradition of such women in popular culture, examining recent examples in the form of comedian Roseanne Arnold and the *Muppet Show*'s Miss Piggy. She suggests that the unruly woman is a crucial figure for feminist theory to contend with, as the relationship between "women and the genres of laughter" has too often been neglected in favor of attention to "the long-standing hold of melodrama on the female imagination" (1995, 4). Instead, the unruly woman offers a rich and pleasurable terrain for feminist readings of popular texts because "the parodic excesses of the unruly woman and the comedic conventions surrounding her provide a space to 'act out' the 'dilemmas of femininity'" (1995, 11). She is frequently marked as fat, rebellious, or caustic, and crucially too she recurrently embraces laughter, making jokes or laughing at herself. In this sense, Rowe observes, the unruly woman informs Mikhail Bakhtin's work on "the carnivalesque," namely that which "contests the institutions and structures of authority through inversion, mockery and other forms of travesty" (1995, 32).

To different degrees and in different episodes, and given their recurrent outspokenness and sexual adventures, all of *SATC*'s female protagonists might be said at one time or another to variously enact the transgressive behavior of the unruly woman. In this respect it is interesting too that so much attention is given to food in the program; all of the women are consistently seen eating, be it at restaurants with their dates, at home alone with take-out, over brunch together, or sharing snacks in the street. In a culture that has taught so many women to fear food, their conspicuous appetites are again refreshingly liberating (even if it could be countered that these scenes make the characters' svelte physiques seem all the more "unrealistic," sustaining bodies that seem part of the program's "fantasy" story world, while underlining again that they are insatiable consumers). Given the link between eating, sexuality, and corporeality, the women's passion for eating is again one of the signs of their unruliness. As the crew's designation of the women's brunches as the "chat-and-chews" and as the centrality of these scenes to *SATC* underlines, talking and eating are closely interlinked; in Rowe's words, "That the unruly woman eats too much and speaks too much is no coincidence: both involve failure to control the mouth" (1995, 37). But I suggest here that it is in the character of Samantha particularly that we see some of the feminist potential and the ambivalence of the carnivalesque "unruly woman" played out in provocative fashion. In laying claim to the (masculine) territory of sexually explicit language and active sexual desire, Samantha co-opts laughter for her own ends, brandishing it as "a weapon of transgression and liberation" (1995, 46) and fueling debates about the program's feminist credentials in the process.

Samantha's persona contains many of the "cluster of qualities" identified by Rowe as characteristic of the unruly woman (1995, 31). While obviously not fat, an "inability to control her physical appetites" is suggested instead by her voracious sexual appetite; her "speech is excessive in quantity, content [*and*] tone" in the manner in which she frequently steers conversation round to her energetic sex life and its breathtaking array of practices, positions, and orgasms. Charlotte continually asks her to lower her voice or moderate her language in these exchanges, simply walking out in disgust at one of their "chat-and-chews" when Samantha announces a propos of nothing, "I'm dating a guy with funky-tasting spunk" (3:39). Her orgasms are excessive not merely in number but also in volume. While Charlotte and Carrie go to the opera one evening, for example, Samantha stays home with her new doctor lover and tries Viagra; as the scene cuts between the friends, her monumental orgasm is aurally matched to the sound of the soprano climaxing in *Aida* (3:37). Similarly, in a later episode, having made advances toward "Friar Fuck" at All Saints Church on the premise of offering her services as a fund-raiser, she later fantasizes about him at home, and as she masturbates the sound of her orgasm is cut to a stirring chorus of "Ave Maria" (4:49). Samantha very much "creates disorder by dominating, or trying to dominate, men," something seen in her insistence that she can "have sex like a man" (1:1). As a result, like Rowe's other unruly women, she is certainly "associated with looseness and [whorishness]" (1995, 31).

Rowe also notes the importance of spectatorial positioning in relation to the unruly woman. She argues that "in acts of spectatorial unruliness, I believe, we might examine models of *returning* the male gaze, exposing and making a spectacle of the gazer, claiming the pleasure and power of making spectacles of ourselves, and beginning to negate our own invisibility in the public sphere" (1995, 12). Ownership of the gaze in *SATC* is ambivalent and not fixed, but contained within this ambivalence is again the potential for a transgressive reading of the women as active subjects. Clearly, their weekly sexual adventures, conspicuous consumption, and attendant construction of themselves as desirable women speak not just to the potential desires of the female audience but also, perhaps, to the objectifying gaze of the male spectator. There is a certain contradictoriness embedded in this perspective, however. First, while Samantha's Pilates-honed body in particular is regularly showcased in the bedroom, Michael Patrick King has observed that the show is not "sexy" as such. In his words, "I think the mistake people make when they categorize our show as dirty or pornographic, which is one of the waves of banners we get thrown, is that nothing about our show is done to titillate you. Nobody's really watching the show to go have sex after it. It's like the last thing you want to do usually after watching an episode of our show" (King 2004). While it would be disingenuous to suggest that the women are not recurrently objectified (indeed, while having a no-nudity clause in her contract, Parker's impossibly trim midriff is heavily fetishized), given the amount of time dedicated to their talking and to their analyzing, comparing, and belittling the sexual performances and other habits of the men in their lives, King may be right to imply that the program does not entirely facilitate a narcissistic male gaze.

Second, the gaze *on* the women is very much accompanied by the active desiring gaze *of* the women. They frequently join together in looking at men and initiate looking at (or commence an exchange of looks with) the men they go on to date or sleep with. In the process they undo the traditional gendering of the shot/reverse-shot system that governs the way men ("active") and women ("passive") generally look at each other in classical cinema and invite not just each other but also the heterosexual female (and indeed gay male) spectator to join them in their transgressive scopophilia. This invitation is staged to spectacular effect in season six when

Samantha decides to boost boyfriend Smith's lackluster acting career and relaunches him as a seminaked model advertising vodka on a massive Times Square billboard, next to the slogan "Absolut Hunk" (6:80). "Fuck me!" remarks Smith when he sees it for the first time, to which Sam dryly replies, "Well, that's the first thing every woman in town will be saying after she sees it." "It's huge!" he continues; "And that's the second," she observes in characteristically unruly fashion.[13]

For Bakhtin, an important element of the carnivalesque was "the grotesque," that which unsettles the "materiality of the body; pursues exaggerated grossness and breaks taboo" and which for Bakhtin was particularly crystallized in the figure of the pregnant, laughing hag (Rowe 1995, 32). A conceptual link here is again suggested by the fact that while Samantha is certainly not "old" per se, she is most definitely singled out as the *oldest* of the friends, a fact that fuels many comic interludes in the program. As Rowe observes, ambivalence is crucial to female unruliness, and historically it carried "charges that were [strongly] positive as well as negative" (1995, 44). Hence, while the program at one level celebrates Samantha's sexuality and desirability as a confident forty-plus woman, at the same time fear of the abjectness of the aging, female body (and the comic possibilities of this) is also written into and onto her. This is evidenced in part by her dread of menopause. In "The Big Time" (3:38), for example, she mistakes a late period for the onset of "the change." As a result she miserably succumbs to the advances of a tiresome middle-aged man, who repulses her with his hip-replacement stories and gray ponytail, only to win a joyful reprieve when her period starts while they're in bed. It seems pertinent, too, here to note that she does eventually become menopausal following her chemotherapy for breast cancer (and suffers other side effects, too, such as hair loss). Furthermore, she is marked as "grotesque" in her efforts to stave off aging with surgery and treatments. A disastrous facial chemical peel, for example, makes her a freakish laughingstock forced to wear a veil at Carrie's book launch (5:71). Later she is panic stricken to find that her pubic hair has started to go gray, and when she chooses to dye it rather than turn into "grandma's pussy," it catastrophically turns a clownish shade of bright orange instead (6:86).

But rather than being only the butt of humor in *SATC*, more than any of the other characters Samantha embraces humor; the sound of her loud, raucous, unapologetic laughter rings out in virtually every episode. It is this loudness, her attendant confidence, explicit language, and sense of entitlement, combined with her active sexuality, that truly marks Samantha as unruly and that leads her to declare audaciously in season three, "Oh, ladies. Let's just say it! We have it all. Great apartments, great jobs, great friends, great sex," before shouting out her window, "You see us, Manhattan? We have it all!" (3:40). (Provocatively, too, "husbands" or "boyfriends" are defiantly and conspicuously absent from this list.) While Kim Cattrall has argued, "All of us are pioneers as comedians with this material," she has noted also that they particularly owe a debt to Mae West, invoking a role model whose sexual persona and command of innuendo in early Hollywood clearly constituted her as another significant historical "unruly woman" (Sohn 2004, 108). So too does Parker's previously mentioned nod to *Absolutely Fabulous* (BBC, 1992–), the British sitcom about the outrageous chain-smoking, booze-fueled antics of public relations guru Edina and best friend Patsy, invoke a more recent example of this model. It has been argued, however, that the use of explicit language in *SATC* was something of a smokescreen, that while superficially it appears daring, it does little in any tangible sense to empower the women (Gill 2007). Nevertheless, in being so resiliently able to laugh at the judgmental strictures of the culture that surrounds her, like her unruly woman predecessors, Samantha refuses to be curtailed or silenced by this culture.

"The First Global Female Epic" or "Feminism-lite"? Public Debate and *SATC*

This provocative subject matter and the portrayal of *SATC*'s four female protagonists quickly became a major discussion point in the media and everyday water-cooler conversation during the series' run. Commentators passionately attacked and defended the show in a debate marked by both its ubiquity and its vehemence. *SATC*'s vision of a postfeminist world as one where women have formed their own support network, are educated and economically independent, but nevertheless recurrently talk about men, sex, and shoes, proved more contentious than Bushnell could ever have imagined. Kathryn Flett was just one critic who attempted to sum up the debate, observing, "Its many critics claim it's trite, cartoony and irritatingly fluffy and girly, but they are probably either sneery blokes or women who don't like the idea that postfeminism might encompass a struggle to reconcile the need for emotional and spiritual fulfilment with the desire for expensive accessories" (2003, 5).

Indeed, a number of male commentators seemed particularly perturbed by the way in which the women talked so frankly together about their sex lives. Paraphrasing Miranda's less than sensitive description of her one-night stand with Steve in "Coulda, Woulda, Shoulda" (4:59), for example, Mark Ellwood observed in *Red* magazine that, "We long for the days when we could date a woman and not worry that she'd pick over the details of our hairy back or droopy foreskin, or tell her mates it was a 'mercy fuck'" (2003, 65). As Flett implies, disagreement centered on whether the women's lifestyles bore any worthwhile relation to the work of gener-

ations of feminism. Was this a program that put female camaraderie, independence, and women's talk on the map of television culture, creating "the first global female epic" in the
process (Wolf 2003)? Was it "feminism-lite" (Bunting
2001)? Or worse, a world where the "heroines spend most of
their time on shopping, cocktails and one night stands" and
are "vapid, materialistic and hysterical" (Orenstein 2003)?

For Orenstein, *SATC* was essentially disingenuous, sup-
posedly celebrating the joys of single life while creating
angst-ridden caricatures preoccupied with "snagging a man"
(2003). And yet the program arguably constructed its protagonists as discerningly single, rather than single and desperate; as Miranda observes in the pilot, "By the time you reach
your mid-thirties, you think, 'Why should I settle?'" Furthermore, the program evidenced that female angst is not the exclusive province of the single and recurrently critiqued the
values of marriage and the aspirations of suburban life. As
Samantha dryly notes in "Don't Ask, Don't Tell" (3:42),
"Marriage doesn't guarantee a happy ending, just an ending."
Witness, for example, not just the longed-for but doomed
"fairy-tale" marriage of Charlotte to Trey that proves to be as
disappointingly glossy and contrived as the pages of *House &
Garden* that inspired it (4:62) but also the behavior of Laney
Berlin. A former party gal from Carrie's crowd, now married,
pregnant, and living in Connecticut, her appearance in an
early episode leaves Carrie, Miranda, and Samantha, at least,
in no doubt that their own single lives are infinitely more
content. In a futile attempt to prove that she has not been de-
voured by the tedium of "settling down," in "The Baby
Shower" (1:10) Laney tries and fails to relive her glory days
by crashing a celebratory "I-don't-have-a-baby" party at
Samantha's house and offering an impromptu strip show.
When her cab comes to take her back to Connecticut, as if
symbolically carting her off to lock her back up, she reluc-
tantly drives away from the life she has left behind, somberly

observing to Carrie, "One day you're going to wake up and you're not going to recognize yourself." Indeed, this same image would be echoed again later in "Anchors Away" (5:67) shortly after Miranda has had a baby, Brady. Samantha packs her off into a cab so that the rest of them can go shopping unencumbered by the motherhood in their midst, while Miranda looks out mournfully at her old (free) life, without her in it. The specter of "desperation" in *SATC*, then, is something women may negotiate whatever their lifestyle choices, the flipside again to the "choices" proffered by third-wave feminism.

Summing up criticisms that the program belittled the preoccupations of modern women, Bignell has observed how "the central characters' fascination with clothes, shoes, hair and personal style is a focus on relatively trivial aspects of women's lives, in contrast to questions of gender equality and the difficulty women face in employment and opportunity" (2004, 166). Similarly, Creeber finds that the program's obsession "with affluence and consumption" creates a narrative world in conflict with the concerns of the previous feminist movement, where "consumerism in all its forms but particularly that which tended to promote a particular view of 'femininity' (such as make-up, fashion, beauty products, women's magazines and so on) were generally perceived as the enemy . . . as instruments of patriarchy" (2004, 145).

However, for Creeber, the women's "self-conscious and ironic use of style" suggests not regression to a prefeminist state but rather a generation of women who, bestowed with an unprecedented array of options, are "discerning, choosy and fastidious about what they want" (2004, 145). Taking issue with Bignell, then, he suggests that *SATC*'s attention to female consumption is more than merely frivolous and may be a crucial element of the ideological challenge it poses, one where feminism is not necessarily compromised by consumption. In his words, "Clothes, shoes and cosmetics may appear 'trivial' to (male) critics like Bignell, but for these four women they represent a world where female desire is now no longer repressed, ridiculed or downgraded" (2004, 148). This sentiment is powerfully evident in "A Woman's Right to Shoes" (6:83) when having visited her old friend Kyra to celebrate the birth of her latest baby (one in a long series of family celebrations thrown by Kyra), Carrie is left bereft when she realizes that her Manolos have been stolen from the hallway. Kyra fails to see why this is a serious matter for Carrie but eventually offers to replace them, until she learns they cost $485. Their conversation continues:

> Carrie: You know how much Manolos cost. You used to wear Manolos.
> Kyra: Sure, before I had a real life. But Chuck and I have responsibilities. Kids, houses. $485? Like, wow.
> Carrie: I have a real life.
> Kyra: No offense, Carrie, but I really don't think we should have to pay for your extravagant lifestyle. It was your choice to buy shoes that expensive.
> Carrie: Yes, but it wasn't my choice to take them off.
> Kyra: They're just shoes.

This leads Carrie to reflect on just how much money she has spent "celebrating" Kyra's life choices. Her various engagement, wedding, and children's parties have cost Carrie more than $2000, yet because *her* life choices as a single woman are not recognized, she gets nothing in return. In her words, "Hallmark don't make a 'Congratulations, you didn't marry the wrong guy' card." She is vindicated when Kyra replaces the shoes after Carrie leaves her a message telling her she is getting married to herself and is registered at Manolo Blahnik. The shoes are not "just shoes," then, but a symbol, not of Carrie's frivolousness but of her right to spend her money as she sees fit in a lifestyle that is as just as valid and worthwhile as Kyra's. Indeed, the show's endorsement of consumerism exists not merely *within* the show but extends to viewers' consumption *of* the show; during its original broadcast, audiences were able to bid for items featured on the most recent episode at auction on the HBO website, while a large variety of *SATC* merchandise ranging from DVDs to martini glasses and umbrellas is still available on the website and in HBO's New York store and has been expanded further still following the commercial opportunities afforded by the 2008 cinema release of *Sex and the City: The Movie*.

I contend, though, that in terms of testing cultural boundaries, *SATC* was at its bravest, at its most divisive, most contentious not when it celebrated female consumption, not when it discussed the finer points of "funky tasting" spunk, not even when it became the first U.S. prime-time program to say the dreaded "c-word" (1:5). Instead, *SATC* arguably pushed taboos most when it dared to imagine a world where "resolutely heterosexual" women (Gill 2007, 244) might be each others' "significant others." As this chapter has discussed, crucially, the program suggested that this homosocial life could coexist with the search for heterosexual sex and romance rather than as a radical alternative to it. It was often this sentiment that led to critics' accusations that the program betrayed feminism, as it continued to devote (many) hours of screen time to talk about men while claiming to be about women. But to feel cheated that the women didn't finally somehow relinquish a life in which men are important to or desired by them in order to satisfactorily evidence their devotion to one another or self-sufficiency outside of men is arguably to disregard what the program did achieve, did capture in its representation of female friendship.

In "The Agony and the 'Ex'-tacy" (4:49), on her thirty-fifth birthday, waiting in a restaurant for her friends, Carrie is left hurt and alone when none of her friends turn up (due to road construction and traffic jams, she subsequently learns from her answering machine). She goes home, feeling desolate, until Charlotte arrives and insists that the four of them go out to the local coffee shop instead. Carrie confesses to them there, "The longer I sat at that table, the more alone I felt. . . . I hate myself for saying this. But it felt really sad not to have a man in my life who cares about me . . . no goddamn soul mate." Miranda reassures her she isn't alone, but it is Charlotte, once again surprising the others and the audience with one of her intermittently disarming comments, who interjects saying, "Don't laugh at me. But . . . maybe we could be each other's soul mates. And then we could let men just be these great, nice guys to have fun with." Samantha replies simply, "Well. That sounds like a plan," and they move on. But the implicit understanding between Carrie and Co. following this dialogue is clear; they are soul mates. And it is in such moments—in the program's consistent thread that, while acknowledging the women's wish to have boyfriends and lovers, never loses sight of the love they have for one another—that *SATC* was ultimately at its provocative best.

Chapter 3

New York Stories

Representation and the City
in *Sex and the City*

The representation of women and of sex in *SATC* was widely
felt to be so provocative for a television series when the program appeared that these subjects predictably came to dominate discussion of it. As a result, numerous other significant
themes that also warranted attention rarely received it in either academic or media coverage. In this chapter I tackle
some of these other arenas more extensively. After examining *SATC*'s claim to have constructed four female "archetypes," I explore the show's status as a "queer" text and its
representation (or absenting) of class and racial difference.
In addition, I also look more closely at the representation of
New York itself, because while the "sex" of *Sex and the City*
has been widely analyzed and commented on, "the city" has
gone rather more neglected.

"Which *Sex and the City* girl are you?" *SATC*'s Female Archetypes

The endless media and audience attention given to scrutiniz-
ing *SATC*'s women protagonists demonstrates just how
much they fueled the public imagination. Darren Star and

his team astutely constructed four divergent women who acted as foils for one another, each of them representing different versions of thirtysomething single womanhood, albeit all of them white, conventionally attractive, and upper middle-class. Star has commented, "For me the important thing about the women in *SATC* is that they were all women in their 30s and had probably had opportunities to get married and had chosen in some way, shape or form to be single. And so [the program] was looking . . . at *what the archetypes of those women would be*" (Star 2004, emphasis added). In his words, these archetypes emerged as Miranda, "the working woman" with a cynical edge; Charlotte, the optimistic and romantic "rules girl" following old-fashioned formulas designed to win an eligible husband;[14] Samantha, "the woman who . . . came of age in the 70s and had a really free approach to sex"; and Carrie, arguably less of an archetype and more of an "everywoman," who acted as "the prism through which the women collected their experiences . . . sort of all of them" (Star 2004). These archetypes evidently struck a potent chord with audiences, as discussing which one of the characters one most resembled soon became a stock conversation among female fans (see Jermyn 2004), while endless magazines, as well as the show's website, invited readers to take quizzes determining "Which *Sex and the City* girl are you?" (cf. *heat,* January 19, 2002).

The currency of these archetypes was evident in more cerebral circles too, when the best-selling self-help/coaching guide *The Mind Gym* used Carrie and Co. to demonstrate four particular personality types and their different kinds of motivation, in an exercise titled "Understanding People: The *Sex and the City* Way" (*Mind Gym* 2005, 91). With Charlotte designated "the carer," Samantha "the driver," Miranda "the professional," and Carrie "the adapter," *The Mind Gym* suggested that through grasping the complexities of these types the reader would be able to effectively "adapt [his or her] behavior to fit with the other person's motivation" and "get the best" out of each of them (2005, 97). The fact that the book adopted *SATC*'s protagonists in order to explore this theme demonstrates both the extent to which the characters worked effectively as contrasts to one another and the extent to which they were known broadly to an expansive audience made up of both men and women; *The Mind Gym* aims to appeal to a wide readership, not merely to be a "women's" book.

Star's archetypes also clearly intended to address some of the different responses to third-wave feminism felt among contemporary women and to embody some of its concomitant dilemmas. While Star denotes Charlotte as a "rules girl," in fact she often seems deeply conflicted about these rules. Caught between tradition and the new feminist order, she clearly feels compelled by social convention to try and follow them but crucially never quite remains won over by them, arguably in part because they evidently deny her sexual needs (hence "All my rules just went out the window," she says after sleeping with film star Wylie Ford shortly after meeting him [2:22]). Intermittently undermining her WASP persona, she periodically surprises the others with unexpected admissions, such as her fiery affair with a Hasidic Jew in "Secret Sex" (1:6). Yet she has most typically been (mis)represented, somewhat unfairly I would argue, as being merely a prude. In truth, her identity vacillates in this respect somewhat as her occasional disclosures over "chat-and-chews" with the others disarm them and suggest another more passionate, less conventional side to her that is repressed by "the rules." After all, not only is it Charlotte who suggests to the other women that they (and not her husband) are her soul mates but also she is able to instruct Miranda in the art of talking dirty ("The Awful Truth" [2:14]) and leaves her straightlaced former sorority friends aghast over lunch when she asks, "Don't you ever want to be pounded hard? . . . Dammit,

I just really want to be fucked you know, really fucked" ("Frenemies" [3:46]).

Meanwhile, high-powered, Harvard-educated lawyer Miranda battles to have her independence and success accepted by others, for example, tiring of having to continually justify her "single-woman" status when she buys her first apartment ("Four Women and a Funeral" [2:17]). Consequently she sometimes overcompensates and struggles to accept help from other people or do anything that might compromise her independence, particularly when faced with the prospect of becoming a mother and, later, a wife. Samantha lives by her own "rules," determined to meet men on a level playing field, both sexually and professionally, devoid of maternal interest and making no apologies for it. Carrie, as many commentators have observed, has qualities drawn from each of them. By creating these contrasting types and a lead protagonist who amalgamated them all, *SATC* successfully constructed a program rich in opportunities for multiple points of audience identification. With these various outlooks in place, it was able to facilitate an endless debate, both textually and extratextually, comprised of different perspectives on women's lives under third-wave feminism.

Perfectly Queer Television?

In addition to this woman-centeredness, *SATC* was also marked by a particularly queer sensibility, being littered with transgressive moments and storylines that undermined normative categories of gender and sexuality. Indeed, arguing that this was a central feature of the program, Jane Gerhard has suggested that *SATC*'s remarkable success can in fact be attributed to the manner in which it managed to coalesce "two related trends in recent popular culture: postfeminism and queerness" (2005, 37). She notes, for example, that the women's dependence on and intimacy with each other, superseding their relationships with the men in their lives, constructs "an elective family structure [that] gay men and lesbians have relied on for generations . . . an alternative that by its very existence, grants the women options different from those traditionally signified as 'heterosexual'" (2005, 44). As the last chapter discussed, this sense of an "elective family" was bolstered by Star's consciously avoiding giving the women any real sense of personal or family history; only very rarely do we hear them refer to any blood relatives and, barring Charlotte's brother who appears briefly in season two, we are never introduced to any of them.

In an interview, actress Cynthia Nixon has made much the same point as Gerhard, remarking that "*SATC* is about how important friendships are when you're not married and don't have a family. It's a gay thing, and a single-person thing, where your friends are your family" (cited in Sohn 2004, 86). The characters evidently self-identify this way. For example, when learning that Miranda has decided not to terminate her pregnancy, Charlotte delightedly responds, "*We're* having a baby!" ("Coulda, Woulda, Shoulda" [4:59]), while it is Carrie who comforts Samantha through the flu and administers her mother's childhood cough remedy to her in "All or Nothing" (3:40). Structurally, then, and particularly potently in an era where in the United States the Bush administration is giving ever more support to endorsing and funding promarriage legislation and support groups, the figure of the single woman and the gay man bear some comparison, as both are placed as "outsiders" in respect to the heteronormativity of traditional family and marriage. It is not only *SATC*'s women who are conscious of social pressure to be married; in "The Turtle and the Hare" (1:9) we learn that Stanford's grandmother has effectively disinherited him because he will only receive his bequest from her if he ties the knot, leading him and Carrie to consider a marriage of convenience.

Beyond its vision of an alternative family structure, and aside from the importance of Stanford and Anthony as its

"GBFs" (Gay Best Friends), *SATC*'s frequent use of camp "insider" references (cf. multiple nods to *The Wizard of Oz* in "The Baby Shower" [1:10], "Evolution" [2:23], "Politically Erect" [3:32], and "The Real Me" [4:50]), camp humor and performances, "gay" vernacular (cf. the recurrence of the word *fabulous*), and its sexually liberal politics have all been read as playfully queer, forming another arena through which the program, superficially at least, destabilized traditional binaries and gendered roles. Alessandra Stanley, writing in the *New York Times*, for example, was one of numerous commentators to note that, in particular, "the rakish sexual voracity of Samantha . . . [hints] at the show's sexual inversion. Samantha has all the traits of a promiscuous gay man, very thinly disguised as a P.R. woman" (2003, 1). Indeed, in "Old Dogs, New Dicks" (2:21), while at a Drag Queen Bingo night, Samantha bumps into Brad, an old conquest and former semiprofessional hockey player, who in homage to her has apparently abandoned such hypermasculine pursuits and morphed into a drag queen named Samantha. Later, in season four, she abandons heterosexuality, albeit only temporarily, for a lesbian relationship with Brazilian artist Maria.

If "tri-sexual" Samantha (cf. her declaration that "I'll try anything" [3:34]) is the character most overtly marked as queer, other quintessentially queer moments and themes abound in relation to the other protagonists too. Indeed, the first time we see all the women together (1:1), they are being served cake by a particularly garishly attired collection of drag queens singing "Happy Birthday" to Miranda. In "Bay of Married Pigs" (1:3), inverting the societal norm that has long pressured gay men and women to "pass" as straight in order to conform, Miranda, decked in suit and tie, "passes" for lesbian in order to secure an invite to a dinner party at her boss's house. Later, in "Boy, Girl, Boy, Girl . . ." (3:34) Carrie dates Sam, a younger man whom she subsequently learns is bisexual, and at a party with him she also shares a brief lesbian kiss with his friend Dawn (played by that episode's star cameo performer, Alanis Morrisette). Meanwhile, the typically girlish Charlotte cross-dresses as a man for Baird Johnson, a photographer showing an exhibition at her gallery titled "Drag Kings: The Collision of Illusion and Reality." Charlotte finds herself strangely aroused by the role-play when she poses for him and, discovering a hitherto unexplored "masculine" sexual assertiveness, she makes the first move, initiating sex with him. At the gallery too, on realizing he has been admiring a picture of a woman dressed as a cowboy, Stanford undoes the gendered binaries of sexual identity, gay and straight, when he exclaims, "Oh my God! I'm attracted to her! Maybe I'm a lesbian!"

However, David Greven has argued that the program only superficially appears to embrace a "gay sensibility" and "queer life" (2004, 40), ultimately keeping these themes at its periphery. He notes that in the "Boy, Girl, Boy, Girl . . ." episode in particular, it constructs a "triumphantly phobic parade of sex freaks" (45) where bisexuality is toyed with and pondered before being rejected when Carrie walks out on Sam at the party. Interestingly, Ros Gill focuses on the same episode to make precisely the same point, concluding, "For all its 'frank' and 'liberated' sex talk," and not "withstanding its regular flirtations with lesbianism and bisexuality, it is resolutely heterosexual and phallic" (2007, 244).

What both Greven and Gill seem to rather privilege here, however, is the operation of "closure," implying that resolutions efface or negate the ambiguities, actions, and digressions that precede them. Undeniably, this episode does suggest more than once in patronizing fashion that bisexuality can be seen as a form of immature sexual experimentation, and, undermining her liberal persona, Carrie delivers some surprisingly conservative observations as she discusses Sam's revelation with her friends ("I'm not even sure bisexuality exists"). However, her position is countered by Samantha, who tells her, "I think it's great. He's open to all sexual experiences. He's evolved . . . don't worry about the label." That night Carrie admits, "I couldn't get Samantha's words out of my head . . . maybe gender doesn't even exist anymore," suggesting that Samantha's more progressive position has evidently struck a chord with her. Rather than immediately dumping Sam, the two continue to date, and, chiming with Samantha's estimation, she describes how they go on to have great sex together.

On one level, then, Greven and Gill are both correct to observe that ultimately all the women embrace heterosexuality and, indeed, by the end of the series, coupledom. But this is not to say that the apparently conservative "conclusion," of either this episode or the series as a whole, is what will predominate in the audiences' readings and recollections of the program. Whatever their "final" predilections, the women made inroads never before articulated so frankly on television into exploring and questioning the nature of contemporary sexual mores. As I argue in the next chapter, too, the series end can be read as far more unstable and uncertain than some interpretations have been want to suggest. By the same token, even if heterosexual monogamy is ultimately the place at which the women arrive, as indicated earlier, in the multiple queer moments that have accompanied them en route, *SATC* nevertheless continually highlighted how gendered and sexual identities are in essence performative constructs.

I ♥ NY: *SATC*'s Love Affair with New York

That *SATC* was able to construct and explore such provocative characters and themes was due to a number of contextual factors, including both its place on a nonnetwork channel and a wider cultural moment preoccupied by third-wave

"Who would've thought an island that tiny would be big enough to hold all our old boyfriends?" (Miranda [3:31]). The Brooklyn Bridge, gateway to Manhattan.

feminism and contemporary sexual habits. That it managed to pull it off with such flair was due not merely to the quality of the writing and performances but also to its setting; in the city that never sleeps and where, as Carrie says, "you never know what's just around the corner" (3:48), from its inception *SATC* was, inescapably, a New York story. In what follows, I explore more carefully exactly how New York was able to so unequivocally become the fitting setting for recent television's most celebrated depiction of the lives and loves of contemporary, urban women and to ask exactly whose vision of New York it popularized.

Alongside their friendships with one another, the city in *SATC* forms the mainstay of its protagonists' lives. Carrie's voiceover recurrently opens with a gem of wisdom, sometimes celebratory, sometimes jaded, but always heartfelt, about what New York and New Yorkers are like. "There are some things I love about New York," she tells us at the start of "The Caste System" over an evocative montage of idyllic scenes in Central Park (2:22): "that week in spring when it's warm but not hot and trees are just beginning to bloom, men in suits, three papers and twelve gossip columns." More precisely, it is Manhattan the women adore; Miranda's move to Brooklyn following marriage to Steve prompts much soul searching as she struggles with the prospect of joining the "bridge-and-tunnel" crowd (a fear that seems to be marked as much by anxieties about class as about commuting). In sum, the romance of *Sex and the City* is not just set *in* the city, it is *with* the city.

The title of the winter 2001–2 season 4 finale, "I Heart NY" (4:66), made this sentiment plain. This strangely prescient episode, which was apparently written by Michael Patrick King prior to the terrorist bombing of the World Trade Center on September 11, 2001 (Sohn 2004, 144), enacts a moving love letter to New York as Carrie insists she take Big out on one final date in/with the city before he moves to California, telling him, "You owe it to us. And by us I mean New York and myself." Evoking the "old time" New York of *Breakfast at Tiffany's* again, they dance at Big's apartment to Henry Mancini's *Moon River*, the film's classic signature music ("Corny," says Carrie; "Classic," says Big). On an evening buggy ride through Central Park ("Corny," says Big; "Classic," says Carrie), she seems overcome by the enormity of the fact that Big could choose to leave. "New York. New York!" she repeats wistfully as if holding the words against herself. "Aren't you going to miss it?" This episode wasn't screened in the United States until February 10, 2002, however, and given this timing it seems likely that, as Jim Smith puts it, a little "editorial surgery" was performed on it prior to broadcast (2004, 266). At the very least, a moving dedication was added to the end credits that articulated the real sense of affection the cast and crew felt for their living set: "To our city of New York . . . then, now and forever."

In the newly written material following September 11 (after which the image of the World Trade Center had been removed from the opening credit sequence), the series' devotion was made explicit again in the first episode of season five, "Anchors Away" (5:67), when a newly single Carrie declares that from now on the city is "her boyfriend." As New York fills with sailors during Fleet Week, itself an apparent intertextual nod to one of the most celebrated and joyful of New York movies, *On The Town* (1949), Carrie embarks on a series of dates not with any man but with the city itself. Ironically including a trip on her own to Paris cinema to see *Joy for Two*, in essence this episode articulates that Carrie's love affair with New York supersedes that of any man. As she observes: "You're never alone in New York, it's the perfect place to be single. The city is your date." From the opening nighttime high-angle shot of Carrie skipping past the Plaza Hotel, which then flamboyantly dollies down to street level and back up to settle on the awning of the Paris cinema, the episode is rich in location shooting. It features numerous shots of the women out walking the streets of Manhattan, including a glorious sequence of their sashaying through Times Square dressed to the nines as they go to meet their sailors, with the city dazzlingly lit behind them. The mood is optimistic but somber, like the popular image of the post–September 11 city itself, as Carrie grapples with the question, "When it comes to being carefree single women, have we missed the boat?"

Darren Star has told how, from the outset, "It was really important for me that the show was shot in New York and HBO was really supportive of that" (Star 2004). He was determined too to secure Sarah Jessica Parker for the lead, an actress whose appropriateness for the role was in part embedded in her star persona as a dyed-in-the-wool New Yorker and an actress who recurrently refers in interviews to her love for the city.[15] The decision to film in New York was embedded too in Star's wish to do something cinematic and nonnetwork: "I wanted to create a show that [glamorized] New York. Because I felt that New York was just a really exciting, glamorous city that hadn't really been perceived that way on television for a long time . . . [like] the world of *Vanity Fair*" (Star 2001). The representation of the city, then, was crucial to how *SATC* blended its particular fusion of fantasy and realism. Star's representation of Manhattan synthesized an escapist edge on the one hand (e.g., granting the protagonists apparently limitless leisure time to explore its riches, alongside knowledge of every new trend and hotspot), with a commitment to authenticity on the other (e.g., consistently shooting on location).

Romance and Realism: *Sex and the City*'s Fantasy Island

Unlike other contemporaneous New York or urban sitcoms such as *Mad About You* (ABC, 1992–99), *Friends*, or *Seinfeld*

"I wanted to create a show that [glamorized] New York" (Darren Star). The lights of Times Square glitter behind the women in "Anchors Away" (5:67).

that were overwhelmingly restricted to sets in their recon-structions of city space, every episode of *SATC* not only fea-tured scenes of Carrie walking Manhattan's streets but also referenced real bars, real street names, real restaurants, and real districts and showed the female protagonists *really* within them. In this sense it was unlike its woman-in-the-city precursors, such as *That Girl* and *The MTM Show*, which removed their heroines from the actual city after the opening credits. The show's authenticity in this respect is underlined by the availability of *SATC* maps of New York, where one can plot one's own journey through the New York frequented by the women, included, for example, in Akass and McCabe (2004) and Sohn (2004) and on the HBO website and the "*Sex and the City* Hotspots" bus tour run by On Location Tours (www.screentours.com). Furthermore, just as it tapped into the zeitgeist of third-wave feminism, *SATC* acknowledged real issues and trends happening in the city in this period, for example, jokes about Mayor Giuliani's less than open-minded policies (3:34) or Samantha's move to the Meatpacking District (3:36) following its rapid gentrification at this time. Dramatically, the use of vox pops with "random" New Yorkers on the streets, many of them evidently not from the upper middle-class milieu of Carrie and Co., also added to this sense of the program's being embedded in the city space.

But while being inescapably "real" in one sense, as a space loaded with iconic memory and nostalgia, *SATC*'s New York is also seen to proffer transformative, magical qualities. This is particularly true of Carrie, who as *SATC*'s storyteller opens numerous episodes with the age-old words, "Once upon a time" and who often appears to be the princess at the center of her own enchanted story, a motif signaled from the start in the girlish fantasy-style tutu she wears in the opening credits. In "Where There's Smoke" (3:30), for example, the fairy-tale theme comes to the fore when Carrie meets a new politician boyfriend, Bill, at a New York City Fire Department charity event on Staten Island. Having posed the question, "Do all women just want to be rescued?" she finds herself rendered the Cinderella of a "Staten Island Ferry Tale" when she runs for and misses the last boat back to Manhattan at midnight, losing one of her (Jimmy) "Choos" in the process. While playfully suggestive of a make-believe world, this episode nevertheless includes authentic and beautifully shot location footage of the women crossing the Hudson River. As the Statue of Liberty glows in the night sky behind them and the lights of New York glitter, it isn't difficult to imagine Manhattan as "a magical island" (1:8). While *SATC* co-executive producer John Melfi has said that they sought to avoid merely a "touristy version" of the city (Sohn 2004, 146), scenes like these call to mind the New York of the romantic, cinematic popular imagination—of Woody Allen's Queensboro Bridge admired against a Gershwin soundtrack in *Manhattan*, of Holly Golightly's dawn escape to 5th Avenue in *Breakfast At Tiffany's*—and leave one wondering where the New York of fantasy ends and the "real" one begins. Elsewhere, in one of many fairy-tale images, when Petrovsky miraculously manages to summon up the means to take Carrie on a Narnia-style, romantic, moonlit sleigh ride through the snow in Central Park, neither she nor the viewer question how (6:92).

On this small island that well over a million people call home, and where the population swells and multiplies with visitors and commuters every day, the promise of adventure is always in the air, with an infinite number of stories and the possibility of romance written into its very fabric. *SATC* draws on and extends the romantic heritage of New York—a heritage that is both literary and peculiarly cinematic—as a place of endless narratives, endless pleasures, and, crucially as I now explore, a refuge for female flânerie. In this way, *SATC* constructs the city itself as a kind of cameo performer, until it comes to comprise what Sarah Jessica Parker has potently described as the program's "fifth lady" (cf. *Larry King* 2004).

Courting "the Fifth Lady": The Gendered City of *SATC* and the Flaneuse

Despite the fact that it is something of a cultural commonplace to refer to cities as "she," in many ways it is curious that Parker genders the city this way, especially as in "Anchors Away" (5:67) Carrie had referred to it as "her boyfriend." Designating the city as "the fifth lady," Parker unproblematically endows it with a feminine identity and aligns it with the four female protagonists, constituting their

A place of infinite stories and endless romantic possibilities—"Our city of New York . . . then, now, and forever" (4:66).

other gal pal. In part, this seems out of keeping with the New York of the popular imaginary, as elsewhere the city is enduringly associated both with the aggressive streets of pre–Rudy Giuliani urban fallout (perhaps most memorably captured on film by director Martin Scorsese) and with the masculine cut-and-thrust world of commerce and industry (as crystallized in the media's well-worn frenetic images of the New York Stock Exchange, where Carrie brings her feminine charms to bear in "To Market, To Market" [6:75]). This "dark" vision of New York also has a history in television drama, both predating and contemporaneous to *SATC*, as seen in programs such as *NYPD Blue* (Fox, 1993–2005) and *CSI: New York* (CBS, 2004–). But echoing Star's earlier comments, Parker has observed of the show's aesthetic that "we were shooting it *in a way that the city hadn't been shot*, you know, sparkly and pretty" (Sohn 2004, 14, emphasis added). Certainly, *SATC* overflows with exquisite nighttime photography of New York, such as the night at the opera where Carrie swoons into Petrovsky's arms outside the illuminated fountains of Lincoln Center ("The Ick Factor" [6:88]). Coming straight back to earth with a bump, though, moments later this romantic vision of New York is replaced by the "real" one when Carrie insists they go for supper at McDonald's.

More broadly, Parker's feminization of the city is intriguing because much of contemporary popular culture continues to construct the city as a space where women are at risk, while Elizabeth Wilson has shown that historically "the sophisticated urban consciousness" of the nineteenth and early twentieth centuries "was an essentially male consciousness" (1991, 5). In particular, and central to existing critical work on the representations of the city, the figure of the flaneur, or city stroller, celebrated in the writings of French poet Charles Baudelaire and German cultural critic Walter Benjamin, has overwhelmingly been read as male. Briefly I want to establish

"We were shooting it in a way that the city hadn't been shot . . . sparkly and pretty" (Sarah Jessica Parker). The illuminated fountains of Lincoln Center where Carrie swoons into Petrovsky's arms in "The Ick Factor" (6:88).

the cultural significance of the flaneur in order to explore how *SATC*'s depiction of women owning urban space was so significant.

Reaching his zenith in Paris in the mid-nineteenth century, the flaneur was a man with both the time and the financial means to indulge penchants for fashion and city loitering, one who relished, in Wilson's words, "the kaleidoscope of urban public life" (1991, 5). Essentially a voyeuristic figure, the flaneur has been understood as a man who observed city life without interacting with it, moving freely across its manifold spaces. But, as Wilson notes, the new urban consciousness was also marked by sexual anxiety and a preoccupation with sexuality outside of the family: "This in itself made *women's very presence in cities a problem*" (1991, 5; emphasis added). In the figure of the flaneur, the freedom of the city, the right to walk it, became conceptualized as male. A woman undertaking the same perambulations could expect to be taken for a prostitute (as Carrie is on more than one occasion) and signaled disorder, hence Wilson's famous appellation that woman constitutes a troubling "sphinx in the city" (1991).[16]

Yet as Wilson also notes, even in the earliest moment of this growing urban culture, there was a paradox, a contradiction in the gendering of the city as a male playground. Despite the constraints placed on women's autonomy of movement there, the city emancipated them more than rural life or suburban domesticity. In the greater diversity of its composition, the city offers women at least a kind of freedom and is not only male in its gendered contours; in Wilson's words, "Male and female 'principles' war [against] each other at the very heart of city life. The city is 'masculine' in its triumphant scale . . . it is 'feminine' in its enclosing embrace, in its indeterminacy and labyrinthine uncentredness" (1991, 7). It is this ambivalence that allows the city of *SATC* to be both its "fifth lady" and Carrie's "boyfriend."

It is also in part this paradox and the growth of consumer culture—as shopping legitimated women's entry into public space and endowed them with greater freedom of movement—that subsequently, however hesitantly and contentiously, enabled the critical and cultural possibility of a flaneuse, a female loiterer and devotee of urban vibrancy. It is this vision, of a female-centered, female celebration of city life, that *SATC* embraced. Throughout the program the persistence of the matrix constituted by femininity, consumption, and the city is continually foregrounded in the women's seemingly endless shopping trips, cocktail nights, and brunches. But the city is also a space where we often see them simply stroll contentedly without any obvious sense of destination. As Catherine Fowler (2007) has observed,

"Wandering creates a space for wondering"; hence Carrie enjoys her urban perambulations for the valuable space they afford her to think. Helen Richards has argued that Carrie incontrovertibly constitutes a "visible *flaneuse* for the postmodern era" (2003, 155) and that this status is immediately signaled by the opening credits of the program. This montage features snapshots of New York architectural icons such as the Chrysler Building and the Brooklyn Bridge, intercut with images of Carrie looking about her, smiling knowingly (not unlike Wilson's sphinx, perhaps) and moving confidently through the streets of Manhattan, before a bus adorned with her own image advertising her newspaper column drives past. As Richards (2003) notes, with its emphasis on her eyes, the sequence clearly shows Carrie's gaze on, ownership of, and pleasure in the city, while in a similar vein, Akass and McCabe argue that the montage "grants her subjectivity and a unique perceptual access to the metropolis" (2004, 178).

That this "perceptual access" is granted to our heroine in New York is not happenstance; as the preeminent city of U.S. modernity, New York forms a logical and historically accurate home to the American flaneuse. The program draws on and extends the connections that have long existed between the image of New York, the urban woman, and consumerism. By the second half of the nineteenth century, the area extending from Union Square to Madison Square was home to a growing number of splendid department stores where respectable women could go out unescorted, earning it the name "The Ladies Mile." If one of the emergent symbols of modernity was to become the glittering skyscraper, then, so too would its changing vision of femininity and the attendant burgeoning independence of the urban, self-sufficient, single woman.

Countless Hollywood representations of New York, particularly in the romantic comedy genre (Jermyn, forthcoming), ensured that, in cinematic terms at least, it would become known as the most romantic city in the world. Nevertheless, in wider popular and certainly European culture it is still arguably Paris that can lay claim to this title. Indeed, Hollywood has also long held an affection for Paris, and the city's romantic status is explicitly explored by *SATC* in its two final episodes. In "An American Girl in Paris: Part Une" (6:93), another title that makes an intertextual nod to *SATC*'s cinematic heritage, Carrie gives up her life in New York to move to Paris and be with her artist boyfriend, Aleksandr. On arrival, in a knowing exchange, his daughter asks Carrie if it's her first time in Paris, and she replies animatedly, "Well, not if you include the movies." Carrie's response playfully acknowledges some of the heavily romanticized images that follow, such as the moment when (wearing her own flamboyant take on a classic Breton black-and-white striped sweater) she excitedly steps out among the red flowers adorning her Hotel Plaza Athénée balcony into a picture postcard shot of the Eiffel Tower. But these final episodes also undercut the popular romantic vision of Paris. Soon after her arrival (6:94), a montage played out against melancholic and typically "French-style" accordion music shows Carrie pursuing flânerie in her newly adopted city. In one scene she smokes a cigarette in a patisserie, while eating from a table filled with an impressive array of sweet delights. But as the camera pans left we realize that, oddly, her nearest companion is a particularly jowly and somber-looking dog, and the image becomes a disconcerting one of isolation. Afterward, strolling the cobbled streets, she smiles at a sweet-looking child held aloft on her father's shoulders, but as they pass by the girl unceremoniously smacks Carrie on the head. Adding insult to injury, Carrie then moans in horror when she realizes she has ruined her white Christian Louboutin shoes by treading in some Parisian dog mess.

What is intriguing about this sequence is the way Carrie

patently "fails" to be a flaneuse, in this, the very city that gave rise to flânerie. One disastrously comical and lonely incident follows another, suggesting both Carrie's ingrained identity as a New Yorker and even perhaps the urban cultural primacy of New York. Interestingly, in formulating her argument that Carrie is indeed a flaneuse, Richards describes Carrie as a "detached" figure, primarily because she is repeatedly single in the series (2003, 153). Yet I would argue that it is only really here, in Paris, away from her friends and her city, that we ever truly see Carrie as detached. Richards's somewhat misleading phrase neglects the degree to which Carrie is a *participant*, is active in and not merely *observing* New York—her beloved—City. It does not merely "flow past" her, to borrow Baudelaire's phrase (cited in Richards 2003, 150), and in this sense Carrie both enacts and outstrips the position of the flaneur. While her column requires her to maintain a reflective persona, rather than being "detached" from this city, Carrie generates stories in it—she is sought out to contribute to them as well as to report them; she engineers events as well as relates them; she is constructed as a protagonist in New York, as *in* its story, and in this sense she is unlike the aloof historical figure of the male outsider/observer flaneur. Like Bushnell, as Nancy Franklin has observed of the original column, she is "both voyeur and participant" (1998, 74). This hybrid identity is perhaps suggested by another recurrent visual motif in the program, namely the image of Carrie looking out from her apartment window. Frequently used as a means of framing the "think-and-types," the camera often wanders into and out of Carrie's window and pictures her sitting there writing her column, an image that arguably crystallizes her insider/outsider status, while the reflection of the glass parallels her role as reflective narrator.

Nevertheless, the implication that flânerie continues to pose a "problem" for women is still present in *SATC*, embed-

A New York flaneuse: Carrie strolls the city in the opening credits but, in an ambiguous moment, gets splashed in the process.

ded from the start in the opening credits. In the ambiguous moment at the end where Carrie is splashed by the bus, it seems as if she is humiliated by her own image, knocked back or belittled for having mistakenly thought that these streets were hers for the taking, a "punishment" that also carries with it disconcerting sexual connotations. As we saw in the last chapter, *SATC*'s opening credits pay homage to those of its "woman-in-the-city" precursors *That Girl* and *The MTM Show*, the latter sequence famously ending with Mary triumphantly tossing her hat into the air. Hence it is strangely disconcerting that *SATC*'s credits end on a comparatively dark note, perhaps highlighting how this series will both embrace the city and show moments of ambivalence about it, for, with its "toxic bachelors," urban street noise, and overpriced apartments, New York can sometimes be wearing too. Thus all these credits point to one of the particularly problematic markers of flânerie for women: a woman can never (or rarely) take up the role solely of voyeur or be merely observer. As Carrie walks the city she is also very much situated as spectacle, as *object* of the gaze, a motif highlighted in the credits by her incongruous tutu, the stare of the passing Japanese tourist with a camera round his neck, and her picture on the passing bus. In this sense *SATC*'s credits both celebrate the figure of the flaneuse and suggest some of the conflicts she embodies.

Yet Parker was right to imply that *SATC* genders the city as feminine. While much of the media continues to perpetuate a culture of peril for women that instructs them to instinctively fear the city, *SATC* constructs a metropolis in which the absence of urban danger for women is refreshingly and conspicuously liberating. They can go to bars alone, travel at night, and date strangers without compunction. Even when Carrie is mugged (3:47), she never really seems terribly threatened by the experience, and what her assailant really wants most is her shoes.

Absence and Diversity: The Lost City of New York

Of course, Carrie and Co. predominantly move in the circles of Manhattan's elite and rarely venture into or encounter the New York of its "underclass," the housing projects, the ghettoes, or indeed the city's less salubrious suburban outposts. Their trip to Staten Island when Carrie is a judge for the annual FDNY calendar competition constitutes a considerable excursion. When a shivering Charlotte complains on the ferry that the competition could have been held on Manhattan because "they have firemen on the Upper East Side too, you know," Carrie points out that it is class snobbery rather than the chill air that is fueling Charlotte's disgruntlement, when she replies, "Yes, I know they do, sweetie, and they only put out the really top-notch fires." On arrival, the island's working-class inhabitants are inherently constituted as "other" to our sophisticated Manhattanites, in the form of the raucous female master of ceremonies dressed in an oversized sweatshirt and the conspicuously overweight black woman judge placed next to Carrie. With its lack of Cosmopolitan cocktails, the absence of smoking restrictions, and the dated music, in Carrie's words, it is like "a quaint European country" (3:31), where the women still have crimped hair and the men "smell of Hi Karate." In this sense, it is important to consider what New York spaces aren't visible in *SATC*, to ask who we don't meet and where the use of location shooting ends. Certainly, the protagonists seldom seem to hazard above the privileged Upper East Side or off Manhattan.

This is not to say that *SATC*'s narrative arcs entirely sidestep class issues. For example, Miranda and Steve initially struggle to make their relationship work given the apparent incompatibility of his working-class-bartender-from-Queens status and her position as a high-flying Manhattan lawyer. Steve ends their relationship the first time around when he realizes that she's "going places" while he can't afford to buy a suit in order to accompany her to one of her corporate functions ("The Caste System" [2:22]). But this conflict is as much about gendered inequities as classed ones (*she* is the primary breadwinner) and is diffused when he eventually goes into business with Aidan, and they buy a bar. In terms of race, musically the series seems to open with the promise of a culturally diverse city in its use of Douglas J. Cuomo's lively salsa-style theme, but like the disappointingly narrow breadth of representation that follows, it is "salsa-lite," apparently produced with a predominantly white audience in mind. In sum, this is indeed a rarefied, largely Caucasian, materially advantaged vision of New York where class and ethnic diversity is generally glimpsed only on the margins of the protagonists' privileged world, and it is this absence that is arguably the most problematic aspect of *SATC*'s representation of New York.

Not until season six, for example, is there anything like a regular African American cast member in the series, when Miranda meets and eventually starts to date the handsome new tenant in her building, Dr. Robert Leeds (Blair Underwood; "A Woman's Right to Shoes" [6:83]). This episode acknowledges the reality of racism, but in playful fashion, when a manipulative Miranda effectively shames her residents' association into accepting Robert's application by suggesting that their misgivings about him are prompted primarily by racial prejudice. Rather than taking this stance on any real moral or legal grounds, however, she does so only because she is attracted to him. With the character of Robert entering the program as late as this, it is difficult not to think that the writers by this time felt compelled to respond to the growing evidence that *SATC*'s New York was overwhelmingly white. Robert is charismatic, accomplished, sensitive. "He is perfect," Miranda admits, but she ends the relationship with indisputably just cause when she realizes that Steve is "the one" and finally finds the courage to tell him she loves him ("One" [6:86]). As a disgruntled fan noted after the end of season four on HBO's *SATC* "What's the Big Deal?" web forum ("bensonj," posted April 30, 2002), "It does not depict New York realistically. Since when did New York become white? . . . Why do I not see any minorities on the show at all?" This troubling question was quashed by the majority of respondents, however, who rather dismissed it with observations such as, "Hey its [*sic*] only a show" ("debbibaron"),[17] thereby evading any real exploration of this discomforting facet of the program.

Prior to Miranda's relationship with Robert, in "No Ifs,

Ands or Butts" (3:35), Samantha had briefly had a black love interest, a successful music artist rep named Chivon. The two are introduced when Samantha is dining with her friends at Fusion, the city's latest fashionable eatery, as he is the brother of Carrie's celebrity-chef and restaurant-owner friend, Adeena. As the two flirt and Samantha hands him her business card, Carrie and Co. all size him up appreciatively before Samantha declares, "I don't see color, I see conquest," thus assuring the audience that none of the women are racist, although they've only had white boyfriends to date. In fact, Samantha is unusually taken with Chivon, even inviting him to stay over after they first have sex. But to Samantha's dismay the relationship is threatened and finally ends when Chivon's sister intervenes by telling Samantha to back off: "I'm sure you're a very nice person. But you're white. And I have a problem with my only brother getting serious with a white woman." This is one of few episodes to explicitly engage with the specter of racism, but it is telling indeed that the racism at stake here is largely that of a black woman's refusal of an interracial relationship within her family. Furthermore, the episode can only deal with the issue in the lightest of fashions; when an outraged Samantha tells her friends about Adeena's outburst over brunch, the conversation is quickly sidelined by the question of whether Carrie should give up smoking for Aidan (cf. the episode's "think-and-type" dilemma, "In relationships, what are the deal breakers?").

In contrast to the apparently prejudiced Adeena, Samantha is more than willing to get to know Chivon, for example, going to a club uptown with him on their first date to hear an act he is considering signing. But in contrast to Carrie's optimistic voiceover, their ultimate incompatibility is signaled here by the connotations of the images of the venue and Samantha's symbolic movement out of the women's more familiar midtown territory. It is immediately apparent on their arrival that the nightclubs Chivon frequents are a world apart from those Samantha is used to. As they walk straight to the entrance past a shout of "Back of the line, mother-fucker!" they are next met by two burly black security guards in front of a metal detector. The guards, and Chivon too, are all dressed in black, blending with the club's dark metallic and black interior, so that Samantha appears all the more in-congruous there. Her blonde whiteness is accentuated fur-ther by her light-colored outfit, consisting of gold jacket and trousers and a tiny crop-top that reveals an expanse of white flesh. The overwhelming image of the nightclub is menacing and far from welcoming, underlining how this "black" world is removed from the spaces the audience is used to seeing Samantha in. Inside the club, Chivon's friends look her over approvingly while Carrie notes in voiceover, "Within a mat-ter of minutes Samantha felt perfectly at home in Chivon's world." Yet the image of her as the only white woman stand-ing in a circle of black men is one of a figure who is anything but "at home."

Samantha initially refuses to submit to Adeena's attempts to warn her off her brother. But later they clash again in a club when Adeena refuses to listen to Samantha's attempts to reason with her, telling her, "I'll say it to you plain. I don't care how many Jennifer Lopez–looking dresses you have hanging up in your closet. You don't belong in here." Their altercation turns into an undignified physical fight, and they have to be pulled apart after trading racial insults ("Get your little white pussy away from my brother!" "Get your big black ass out of my face!"). Samantha finally accepts that the relationship cannot work when Chivon proves unable to stand up to Adeena, evidencing a lack of valor that is a "deal breaker" in her mind. In this way, then, the program appears to have sought to use the storyline to assure the audience that its women protagonists are not racist, while circumvent-ing the prospect of an interracial relationship by attributing its end to an intolerant black woman. Certainly, throughout the series, interaction with peers and professionals drawn from outside the women's own racial group, such as Robert or Chivon and Adeena, or Asian American fashion-show producer Lynne Cameron (Margaret Cho), is comparatively rare.

And yet class, ethnic, and racial diversity does exist in *SATC*, seen in the periphery and cast of frequently nameless extras and cameos that populate the series. It is there in the turban-wearing cab driver who delivers the women across town as they discuss Charlotte's anal sex dilemma in "Valley of the Twenty-Something Guys" (1:4); in the Pakistani busboy who consoles Samantha after she gets stood up by her dinner date in "They Shoot Single People, Don't They?" (2:16); in Sum, the wily Thai house servant who calls the shots in "The Caste System" (2:22); in Jesus, the cleaner at Sam's building in "The Fuck Buddy" (2:26); or in Magda, Miranda's interfering but ultimately endearing Ukrainian housekeeper. What stands out about this list is the consistency with which "other" ethnic and racial groups are frequently relegated to service industry jobs and fleeting supporting roles in *SATC*. At one level, it could be said that, in this way, narratively the program is merely reflecting, though not attempting to scrutinize, the genuine economy of New York as one that thrives on cheap immigrant labor (indeed, in this respect it is telling that when Miranda first has baby Brady she is able to employ not one but two immigrant women as "hired help," Magda and [the silent/silenced because non-English-speaking] Lena [5:67]). It might also be said that the program is merely enacting one of the presumed norms of modern urban "multicultural" life, namely that the majority of people enduringly socialize primarily within their own racial group. And it should be acknowledged also that there are other glimpses of more "positive" ethnically diverse cameo roles: the black woman nurse who Samantha consults about her HIV test (3:41), the Asian vet in "Cock a Doodle Do" (3:48), or the black woman cop who sympathetically allows Samantha to distribute posters defaming her un-faithful ex-boyfriend around his neighborhood (5:67), for example. But *SATC*'s burden of representation in this respect was a significant one, and one that it arguably struggled to adequately address.

That New York performed so perfectly as the location for *SATC* was in part because it tapped into the sense of promise the city has long held in the popular imagination—the belief that "anything can happen here" for anyone—a status and history that is inextricably bound in the city's past as the im-migrant gateway to the United States. *SATC* pivoted on the optimistic spirit of romantic comedy, the belief that, as Car-rie puts it, "We keep trying, because you have to figure . . . there's hope for all of us. Somewhere, out there, there is an-other [who] will love us" (2:14). As I have argued elsewhere, one reason that New York figures so recurrently as the setting for Hollywood's romantic comedies is that the genre con-nects with and perpetuates the city's history as the home of the American dream as experienced through immigration. It constitutes the place where millions of future American citi-zens first set foot on American soil, where they entered the United States with hopes and dreams, romantic and other-wise, of future happiness (Jermyn, forthcoming). The subse-quent spirit of optimism and fortitude embodied by New York—a belief in and anticipation of a better life being possi-ble there, the seemingly limitless potential opportunities that a city so densely populated promises—all of these qualities, which have come to mark the city as the home of a romantic cinematic imagination, are grounded too in its history of im-migration.

SATC makes clear this connection between romantic as-piration and the immigrant dream at the start of "The Freak Show" (2:14). The episode opens with historical black-and-white archive footage of immigrants disembarking at the city, as Carrie says in voiceover, "Manhattan. For millions of our forefathers the gateway to hope, opportunity, and happiness beyond their wildest dreams," before dryly continuing, "Today that hope is still alive. It's called the first date." That *SATC* should both thrive on this set of historical and cultural associations by choosing New York as its setting and seem to efface them through its general lack of engagement with ethnic and racial diversity, then, is at best a lost opportunity, at worst another example of how popular television recurrently fails to adequately address the problems contained within its representational strategies. Here we might turn again to the disaffected words of "bensonj" from the HBO *SATC* web forum, who observed there, "We like to act like we don't condone racism, that it is such a horrible thing. But every time I turn on the television, and I see happy white people, living happy white lives, and a happy white world—I think to myself, boy aren't we racist?"

It is interesting to note too that this issue appeared only relatively rarely in media commentary on the program. The announcement that *SATC*'s sixth season would be its last was another matter, however, giving rise to an immediate flurry of renewed interest in and speculation about the show. In the closing chapter, I reflect on the legacy of *SATC* and the enduring nature of its fandom before looking at some of the controversy that met the last episode. The burden of representation here was again a marked one for the writers: How do you satisfactorily end a topical series that has proclaimed for six years to be about celebrating women's single lives in a culture where "the happy ending" still resoundingly means the formation of a romantic couple?

Chapter 4

Goodnight, Ladies
The Legacy of *Sex and the City*

The final episode of *SATC*, broadcast in the United States on February 22, 2004, and in the United Kingdom on March 19, was met on both sides of the Atlantic with the kind of widespread public and media attention that had come to characterize its run over the previous six years. Public screenings of the final episode, evidence of an "event television" status usually reserved in the United Kingdom for royal weddings and World Cup games, were held in venues such as The Grand nightclub in South West London. In the United States, throughout January and February in New York and Los Angeles, the Museum of Television and Radio ran a series of marathon screening weekends showing all the previous episodes in the run-up to the series finale. Stories abounded of groups of women gathering together to watch the finale collectively with friends, a ritual I too participated in. On a Friday night in a North London living room, along with a half-dozen gal pals and nervously grasping a Cosmo, we braced ourselves for the end.

In the six years leading up to this moment, *SATC* had done more than any other television text preceding it to push back the boundaries governing television's representation of sex and its exploration of female sexuality, language, and the intricacies of female friendship. A number of significant and lauded series with "edgy" qualities that followed in its wake, from *Queer As Folk* (C4, 1999–2000 [U.K.]; Showtime, 2000–2005 [U.S.]) to *Desperate Housewives* to *The L-Word* (Showtime, 2004–; tellingly arriving with the promotional tagline "Same sex, different city") became possible only because of what *SATC* had dared to do and remain indebted to its legacy. Consistently over its six seasons it had raised the bar, too, regarding what an ongoing television "dramedy" might do aesthetically, pursuing a cinematic imagination and the kind of consistently loving attention to location shooting, design, and costume once seen as the reserve of one-off serials and historical dramas. Beyond television, there was a sense that *SATC* had helped make inroads in legitimizing the social value of talk between women, as well as impacting how women talked with one another in the "real world." As Kim Akass remarked in an interview on the eve of the series end, "Women now have a language with which to talk about their experiences and their friendships. It's almost given them permission to have female friendships that are more important than anything else. It has given respectability to something that previously was just gossip— something less than conversation" (cited in Anonymous 2004a).

Evidence of the resilience of the show's impact lives on too in its enduring fandom. Since the program's demise, HBO has maintained an active website dedicated to the show, where at "Shop *Sex and the City*" one can buy a range of merchandise, participate on bulletin boards, vote in polls ("Which look do you like best on Steve?"), download a screensaver, or sign up for the *SATC* newsletter, "The Dish." Some viewers' experience of the show has been able to live on too through "The *Sex and the City* Hot Spots" New York bus tour. Commencing just outside the former Plaza Hotel next to Central Park, where Carrie reenacted her homage to *The Way We Were*, the tour subsequently visits numerous sites that featured in the program. Deftly combining the touristic gaze with fan trivia and consumerism, one can buy a Rampant Rabbit vibrator from the Pleasure Chest or a cupcake from the Magnolia Bakery while watching clips and answering quiz questions, as well as having one's pictures taken at the tour's "pilgrimage spot" (Blau 2007), Carrie's stoop. Georgina Blau, director of On Location Tours, who has been running the excursion daily since October 2001, reports that the number of visitors taking the tour three years after the program's end had remained consistent with its pre-2004 figures, while they actually increased in the period immediately following the series finale.

Rather than only attracting existing die-hard fans, Blau's research shows that a good number of participants on the tour are only moderately familiar with the show and that some 15 percent have never seen it before (Blau 2007). Thus the tour serves both to keep the show "alive" for old viewers lamenting its loss or seeking connection with other fans and to support HBO's continuing commercial interests in the show by attracting new viewers only now discovering it, be that through taking the tour or watching it on DVD or network syndication. Furthermore, in summer 2007 it was finally confirmed after much speculation that a film of the series was going into production. This predictably renewed a whole new flurry of media attention in the series as pictures "leaked" from the set and rumors abounded about the storylines, excitedly filling the pages of a plethora of magazine and newspaper articles. Directed by Michael Patrick King and trailed with a tagline inviting the audience to "Get Carried Away," *Sex and the City: The Movie* triumphantly premiered in London's Leicester Square in May 2008, amid scenes of hordes of celebratory female fans. The film can expect both to be embraced by existing fans and to attract new(er) viewers, while also, of course, opening up a whole new raft of commercial opportunities.

Back in 2003–4, speculation about how *SATC* might and should end had been rife ever since it was announced that season six would be the last ("Will Samantha decide that a monogamous relationship might just suit a woman in her forties? . . . Will Carrie finally capture—or even set free—Big?" [Flett 2003, 6]). The penultimate episode sees Carrie moving to Paris to be with Aleksandr despite Miranda's misgivings and her own pain at leaving her friends, work, and home. But in Paris she is lonely and neglected by Aleksandr, who is consumed by his work as an artist, and their relationship finally breaks up after she tells him uncompromisingly, "I am someone who is looking for love, real love. Ridiculous, unconventional, consuming, can't-live-without-each-other love. And I don't think that love is here." Meanwhile in New York, a bereft Big meets with her friends to seek their counsel on whether he might still save their relationship and if he should go after her, and having won their consent he leaves for Paris. In true Prince Charming style he finds her just when she needs him most, moments after her breakup with Aleksandr, and proceeds to win her back and bring her home. In the final moments of the show leading up to the women's joyous diner reunion, we see where each of the women is in their lives now. We learn that Harry and Charlotte are finally to become parents after being approved to adopt a baby girl in China; having taken Steve's stroke-affected mother into her home and tenderly bathed her after she got lost outside in the wintry streets, the once-aloof Miranda wins the unqualified respect of Magda, who tells her fondly, "What you did—that is love. You love"; Smith flies back unexpectedly early from a film set to tell the formerly resolutely single Samantha that he loves her, and in response she finally admits to him, "You have meant more to me than any man I've ever known"; Big drops Carrie off at her apartment and, coming full circle to reprise the line he delivered there in the first episode, when she asks if he'd like to come up he replies, "Absofuckinglutely."

Unsurprisingly, given its emphasis on romantic union, the final installment of *SATC* was met with mixed reviews, embraced by some for reuniting the friends in their beloved city, but widely seen by others as having disappointingly sold out on the very premise it claimed to have championed as its raison d'être—the celebration of single womanhood. As a program that had promoted itself as endorsing the primacy of female friendship and that had sought to uncover and undermine the myths of heterosexual union on a weekly basis, there was, for many reviewers and audiences, something deeply suspect and sadly predictable about its resolution, a "happy ending" entirely predicated on each of the women's having finally landed Mr. Right. Heated debate ensued on the BBC News website, for example, after readers were invited to comment on the final episode: "I was praying for the end to be Carrie, sat at a café single, still questioning men and women, the future, and Sex and the City, but being OK with being single, and showing that it doesn't detract from being a woman," wrote a disappointed James from the United Kingdom. "After six years of showing women that true acceptance must come from yourself and not from a man, seeing Carrie running back to Big is rubbish," posted an angry Krista from Illinois (BBC News 2004). By ending in this manner, had the series lamentably abandoned its own philosophy? And had all those critics who had all along lambasted the program's double standards and arch conservatism finally been proved right?

Goodbye to the Fairy-Tale of New York

For reasons I will explore by way of conclusion—and as Carrie Bradshaw herself might have been wont to remark—I don't think so.

To complete our journey through this television milestone, I want to revisit the apparent contradictions of *SATC*'s ending and, in doing so, provide a counter response to the charge that the finale betrayed the series' own guiding principles. This critique of the ending failed to contextualize it within the show's history, downplayed its deliberately ambivalent qualities, and neglected its resilient endorsement of the women's relationships with each other and of Carrie's independence at the end. It is a finale that to be fully appreciated has to be read within the narrative arcs, thematic preoccupations, and modes of storytelling that had marked the distinctive style of the program over six seasons.

First, *SATC* was a program that had always pursued and played with the model of the fairy tale and been littered with fairy-tale references, a motif signaled when the pilot began (as did more than one subsequent episode) with the words "Once upon a time." In the stories that followed, for example, after going to the ballet with Stanford, a beguiled Carrie falls in love with *Sleeping Beauty* (1:9) ("You only like it because she gets to sleep a hundred years and doesn't age," he remarks); Miranda reimagines *Hansel and Gretel* by defending the misunderstood witch whose dream house was ruined by a couple of interfering kids (1:10); Carrie fears she will become "The Old Woman Who Lives in Her Shoes" (4:64); the women interrogate the prospect of their being saved by a knight in shining armor (3:30) and continually recount urban myths and dating legends to one another (cf. "The Man, the Myth, the Viagra" [2:20]). Despite its many troubled inhabitants, the "magical island" (1:8) of Manhattan is continually posed as a mystical, enchanted place, "a kingdom far away," as Carrie calls it (1:4), and Big, in her words (4:66), is her (albeit reluctant) Prince Charming within it, a role that his unlikely "rescue" of her in Paris underlines. This sensibility was characteristic of the program's blending of escapist and realist worlds: a world in which four working women never have to turn down a date or a cocktail because of a deadline; a text in which breast cancer sat next to $485 shoes and where an endless string of fabulous designer parties cohabited with IVF failure. There is nothing surprising, inappropriate, or inconsistent, then, in the program's final fairy-tale fantasy, where each of the women finally meets her Mr. Right; because there is also, lurking in the wings of this fairy-tale ending, the sense that this may not be "The End" at all.

Given the continual ups and downs of the ninety-three episodes that preceded it, the endless breakups and makeups between Carrie and Big, and all the women and the men in the friends' lives, it seems somewhat presumptuous to find anything ultimately "final" about this apparent resolution in the world of *SATC*, other than the resilience of the women's friendships. Indeed, underlining the sense of transience often present in the series, it is interesting to note that the 2007 trailer for *Sex and the City: The Movie* featured a voiceover from Carrie, declaring, "They say nothing lasts forever. Dreams change. Trends come and go," with the caveat, "But friendships never go out of style." In the final series episode, a newly returned Carrie enters the diner where her friends await her, and they reunite with shrieks of excitement before they are captured one last time, on the small screen at least, walking out together into the streets of New York. Then, as Carrie completes her final series voiceover in which she ponders the many different guises relationships can take and reflects that paramount among these is the one you have with yourself, a closing montage captures a moment in time seen across the four women's lives. In this sequence the audience is shown an instant of perfect equilibrium for each of them, a glimpse of where they are right now and how the future might look. Charlotte, the WASP who converted to Judaism and adopted a Chinese baby, skips across the traffic with Harry, happily walking their dogs through the Manhattan streets; Samantha gives herself up to romance, makes love with Smith and, rediscovering the lost libido caused by her chemotherapy, starts to climax once again; Miranda, now a wife and mother as well as a high-flying lawyer, laughs with Steve at their family home while they feed Brady; Carrie excitedly, and at long last, takes a call from the formerly commitment-phobic Big who tells her that his house is on the market in Napa.

At this series end, then, the audience recognizes how much each of these women has been through over the course of the previous six years and fleetingly sees each at last joyful and at peace with her life. It is an uplifting sentiment but one that, crucially, is also presented as somehow ephemeral. These are not "scenes" as such, but fragments, as the lack of any dialogue within them (save a few eavesdropped words between Carrie and Big) underlines. The New York of *SATC* had always been one that never stands still, and that sense of time, always moving and passing, is writ large on the aesthetics of the montage, as we pan across each of the women and lose them in quick succession, snatching just a few seconds with each. It wouldn't be cynical to observe that these tableaux are merely moments in time, that there will be more troughs as well as peaks in the arcs that lie ahead, as there always have been. Do we believe Carrie is happy with Big now? Yes. Do we presume that she will be always? No. Unlike Cinderella, the Happily Ever After here comes with definite caveats. But for now, it's perfect.

It would be wrong, too, to suggest that in the series end the women's friendships become secondary to their romantic attachments. Big goes to Paris to rescue Carrie but only after he has won the approval and permission of her friends to "go get our girl" and acknowledged that they, not he, "are the loves of her life." In this exchange, *SATC* once again dared to suggest a world where the love between women friends is the love that shapes their lives the most. Tellingly too, the music chosen to accompany the last scenes is not a romantic ballad

The final episode brings Carrie, her friends, and her city back together again.

but Candy Statton and The Source's inspirational *You Got the Love*, a spiritually charged song about finding strength and surviving in the face of adversity ("Occasionally my thoughts are brave and friends are few, occasionally I cry out 'Lord what must I do?'").

Far from selling out single life at its end, the closing image that the audience is left with encapsulates much of what the series had stood for and celebrated. In its last moments Carrie walks along the crowded streets of New York. She picks up her cell phone, and we learn that Big (finally elevated to a true intimate when he is revealed at last to have a real name, John) is moving back to the city for her. Despite all the criticisms of the finale's abandoning the premise of the single woman, what we are left with, in fact, is exactly that. While Carrie may be on the phone with Big, she is not pictured *with* him in a conventional image of coupledom (her "significant other" has only just been revealed to possess a real name, after all). Rather, "our girl," Carrie Bradshaw, the glorious flaneuse joyfully swinging her bags, is seen back where she belongs, in the urban playground of Manhattan. Tripping along the sidewalks where we have seen her stride a thousand times before, the final image is of a solo, confident, purposeful woman who "[feels like she owns] this city" (1:1). Finally, the surrounding throng consumes her, and she disappears into the crowd, with all its stories, all its possibilities, all its endless promise. And maybe, just maybe, with or without Big but always with her gals, maybe she lives happily ever after . . .

Paris cinema, scene of Carrie's date with the city in "Anchors Away" (6:67). "And maybe, just maybe, she lives happily ever after . . ."

1. Throughout this book, individual episodes will be indicated by noting the season followed by the episode number in parentheses, for example (3:31). Space prohibits me from including an individual episode guide, but a comprehensive breakdown is available in Jim Smith (2004), Sohn (2004), and on the HBO website (www.hbo.com/city).

2. While it isn't immediately obvious from the amount of time she spends with the others at brunch that Miranda has a hugely demanding career, after the birth of her child she has to confront her bosses in order to ensure her hours are capped at fifty-five a week (6:80), and she is regularly pictured working at home.

3. To give this some comparative context again, however, the top-rated cable show during the week of April 4, 2007, was *The Sopranos* (1999–2007) on HBO, going out on a wave of publicity in its last season, which nevertheless attracted "just" 7.662 million viewers.

4. Although in some respects we might also trace it back further still to Rona Jaffe's 1958 novel, *The Best of Everything*, about a group of young women working at a New York publishing company.

5. One notable exception to this is Merck 2004.

6. Carrie later invokes Wharton again in "The Fuck Buddy" (2:26). While admiring the grand brownstone buildings of her neighbor-

hood she tells her date how they make her nostalgic for the New York of Wharton and Henry James.

7. Like *SATC*, *Breakfast at Tiffany's* (1961) and *An Affair to Remember* (1957) share a heritage as texts where the possibility of romance and the New York setting are inextricably linked, with key moments in the drama being played out against the iconic backdrop of Manhattan. *Breakfast at Tiffany's* is alluded to again on numerous occasions (e.g., when Samantha invites Chivon to stay over, having admired his diamond earrings, Carrie's voiceover comments, "She just couldn't resist having breakfast with his Tiffany's" [3:35]) while the women watch *An Affair to Remember* together in "All or Nothing" (3:40). More broadly, with her brownstone apartment, demimonde lifestyle, and penchant for late lie-ins and sleeping masks, there are echoes of the heroine of *Breakfast at Tiffany's*, Holly Golightly, written into the very fabric of Carrie's character.

8. Similarly, in the United Kingdom it was screened on Channel 4, a terrestrial channel generally known for attracting an audience high in the more affluent "AB viewers" beloved of advertisers (Arthurs 2004, 129).

9. The star of *Murphy Brown*, Candice Bergen, would later appear intermittently from the end of season four as Enid, Carrie's hard-nosed editor at *Vogue*.

10. Here *SATC* differed from another significant female ensemble "comedy" show precursor, *Designing Women* (CBS, 1986–93), where characters sometimes sounded as if they were delivering speeches rather than dialogue.

11. In another intertextual nod, Samantha promises "Friar Fuck" she can get Marlo Thomas for a church fund-raiser (4:49), while Carrie also fondly remembers her song, "Free to Be You and Me," in "A Woman's Right to Shoes" (6:83).

12. Also interesting in this respect, however, was *Living Single* (Fox, 1993–98), which featured four young African American women friends, in an apartment block setting that prefigured that of *Friends*.

13. This episode particularly facilitates a queer gaze that extends beyond the women in the audience, as Smith quickly becomes the object of desiring gay fans, something that Samantha confidently and correctly predicts is evidence of his impending celebrity breakthrough.

14. "The Rules" here refers to Ellen Fein's and Sherrie Schneider's hugely successful dating manual, *The Rules: Time-Tested Secrets for Capturing the Heart of Mr. Right* (Warner Books, 1997), published just before *SATC* began. It instructs women on how to follow behavioral guidelines in order to bag a husband (for example, Rule 5, "Don't Call Him & Rarely Return His Calls"). While Charlotte invokes and attempts to abide by these "rules" with varying degrees of success, the series continually questions their whole game-playing premise, as per Samantha's withering observation that "a guy could just as easily dump you if you fuck him on the first date as he can if you wait until the tenth."

15. Although SJP was actually born in Ohio, she moved to New York as a child actress appearing on Broadway.

16. Interestingly, Carrie invokes the same mythology in the pilot episode, noting, "It's like the riddle of the sphinx: Why are there so many great unmarried women and no great unmarried men?"

17. The "What's the Big Deal?" forum is no longer available online, as HBO's *SATC* web archives date back only to 2004.

Akass, Kim, and Janet McCabe. 2004. Ms Parker and the vicious circle: Female narrative and humour in *Sex and the City*. In *Reading Sex and the City*, ed. Kim Akass and Janet McCabe, 177–98. London: I. B. Tauris.

Anonymous. 2004a. A fond farewell. *Guardian*, January 29. http://www.guardian.co.tv_and_radio/story/0,3604,1133644,00.ht ml (accessed January 30, 2004).

Anonymous. 2004b. *Sex and the City* finale draws viewers. http://www.msnbc.msn.com/id/4365502/ (accessed October 31, 2004).

Arthurs, Jane. 2004. *Television and sexuality: Regulation and the politics of taste*. Maidenhead: Open University Press.

BBC News. 2006. Bulletin board discussing final episode of *SATC*. http://news.bbc.co.uk/1/hi/entertainment/3512669.stm (accessed March 15, 2007).

Bignell, Jonathan. 2004. Sex, confession and witness. In *Reading Sex and the City*, ed. Kim Akass and Janet McCabe, 161–76. London: I. B. Tauris.

Blau, Georgette (director of On Location Tours). 2007. Interview by author, New York, April 2.

Bradberry, Grace. 2002. Swearing, sex and brilliance. *Observer*, October 20. http://observer.guardian.co.uk/review/story/0,,815217,00.html (accessed March 15, 2007).

Bruzzi, Stella, and Pamela Church Gibson. 2004. "Fashion is the fifth character": Fashion, costume and character in *Sex and the City*. In *Reading Sex and the City*, ed. Kim Akass and Janet McCabe, 130–43. London: I. B. Tauris.

Bunting, Madeleine. 2001. Loadasex and shopping: A woman's lot. *Guardian*, February 9. http://www.guardian.co.uk/Archive/Article/0,4273,4133655,00.html (accessed September 5, 2002).

Bushnell, Candace. 1994. Swingin' sex? I don't think so . . . *New York Observer*, November 28, pp. 1, 28.

———. 1995a. Downtown babes meet Old Greenwich gals. *New York Observer*, June 12, pp. 1, 27.

———. 1995b. My unsentimental education: Love in Manhattan? I don't think so . . . *New York Observer*, February 13, pp. 6, 1, 17.

———. 1996. *Sex and the city*. London: Abacus.

———. 2000. *Four blondes*. London: Abacus.

———. 2003. *Trading up*. London: Little, Brown.

Carter, Bill. 1998. Rating for *Seinfeld* final grazed Super Bowl country. *New York Times*, May 16, B13.

Chupack, Cindy. n.d. Interview on the HBO *SATC* website. http://www.hbo.com/city/cast/crew/cindy_chupack.shtml (accessed April 11, 2007).

Coren, Victoria. 2003. *Sex and the City* has betrayed us single women. *Evening Standard*, January 3, p. 11.

Creeber, Glen. 2004. *Serial television: Big drama on the small screen*. London: BFI.

Dow, Bonnie. 1996. *Prime-time feminism: Television, media culture and the women's movement since 1970*. Philadelphia: University of Pennsylvania Press.

Ellwood, Mark. 2003. *Sex and the City* ruined my love life. *Red*, February, 65.

Flett, Kathryn. 2002. Review of *Sex and the City*. *Observer*, January 13, p. 14.

———. 2003. I'm still wild about Carrie. *Observer* (Review), July 27, p. 5.

Fowler, Catherine. 2007. The passage between images: The wandering woman from Maya Deren to recent gallery films. Paper presented at the MEDIANZ conference, Victoria University of Wellington, February.

Franklin, Nancy. 1998. Sex and the single girl. *New Yorker*, July 6, pp. 74–77.

Gerhard, Jane. 2005. *Sex and the City*: Carrie Bradshaw's queer postfeminism. *Feminist Media Studies* 5 (1): 37–49.

Gill, Ros. 2007. *Gender and the media*. Cambridge: Polity.

Gray, Jonathan. 2006. Introducing television. *flow* 4 (3). http://www.flowTV.org (accessed August 17, 2006).

Greven, David. 2004. The museum of unnatural history: Male freaks and *Sex and the City*. In *Reading Sex and the City*, ed. Kim Akass and Janet McCabe, 33–47. London: I. B. Tauris.

Griffin, Jennifer, and Kera Bolonik. 2003. The prequel, and sequel, to *Sex and the City*. *New York Times*, June 22, sec. 2, p. 29.

Grochowski, Tom. 2004. Neurotic in New York: The Woody Allen touches in *Sex and the City*. In *Reading Sex and the City*, ed. Kim Akass and Janet McCabe, 149–60. London: I. B. Tauris.

Gurley Brown, Helen. 2003. *Sex and the single girl*. Fort Lee, NJ: Barricade Books.

Henry, Astrid. 2004. Orgasms and empowerment: *Sex and the City* and the third wave feminism. In *Reading Sex and the City*, ed. Kim Akass and Janet McCabe, 65–82. London: I. B. Tauris.

Hoffman, Jan. 2003. Dressing Carrie, right down to those Manohlos. *New York Times*, August 13, B2.

Jaffe, Rona. (1958). *The best of everything*. New York: Simon and Schuster.

January Magazine. 2003. Introduction to excerpt from *Trading Up*, July. http://januarymagazine.com/features/tradingupexc.html (accessed March 15, 2007).

Jermyn, Deborah. 2004. In love with Sarah Jessica Parker: Celebrating female friendship and fandom in *Sex and the City*. In *Reading Sex and the City*, ed. Kim Akass and Janet McCabe, 201–18. London: I. B. Tauris.

———. 2006. "Bringing out the ★ in you": SJP, Carrie Bradshaw and the evolution of television stardom. In *Framing celebrity: New directions in celebrity culture,* ed. Su Holmes and Sean Redmond, 67–85. London: Routledge.

———. Forthcoming. I ♥ NY: The rom-com's love affair with New York. In *Falling in love again: Romantic comedy in contemporary cinema,* ed. Stacey Abbott and Deborah Jermyn. London: I. B. Tauris.

Lambert, Victoria. 2001. Horseplay with a handbag. *Daily Telegraph*, July 4, p. 15.

Larry King Live, CNN. 2004. Interview with Sarah Jessica Parker, February 25.

King, Michael Patrick. 2004. Interview for the Museum of Television and Radio Seminar Series: *Sex and the City* (MTR [NYC] recording ref T:78429 / 059596).

König, Anna. (2004). *Sex and the City*: A fashion editor's dream? In *Reading Sex and the City*, ed. Kim Akass and Janet McCabe, 130–43. London: I. B. Tauris.

Merck, Mandy. 2004. Sexuality in the city. In *Reading Sex and the City*, ed. Kim Akass and Janet McCabe, 48–62. London: I. B. Tauris.

Mercurio, Jed. 2007. Classic twists. *Guardian* (Review section), March 17, p. 21.

Mills, Brett. 2007. *I Love Lucy*. In *Fifty key television programmes*, ed. Glen Creeber, 105–9. London: Arnold.

Mind Gym. 2005. *The mind gym: Wake your mind up*. London: Time Warner Books.

Nelson, Ashley. 2004. Sister Carrie meets Carrie Bradshaw: Exploring progress, politics and the single woman in *Sex and the City* and beyond. In *Reading Sex and the City*, ed. Kim Akass and Janet McCabe, 83–95. London: I. B. Tauris.

Nielsen Media. 2007. U.S. TV weekly audience ratings. http://www.nielsenmedia.com (accessed April 11, 2007).

Orenstein, Catherine. 2003. What Carrie could learn from Mary. *New York Times*, September 5, A19.

Quan, Tracey. 2005. *Diary of a Manhattan call girl*. London: Harper Perennial (special sales edition).

Richards, Helen. 2003. *Sex and the City*: A visible *flaneuse* for the postmodern era? *Continuum* 7 (2): 147–57.

Roberts, Yvonne. 2002. There's more to sex than the facts of life. *Observer*, May 5, p. 30.

Rowe, Kathleen. 1995. *The unruly woman: Gender and the genres of laughter*. Austin: University of Texas Press.

Smith, Jim. 2004. *Manhattan dating game: An unofficial and unauthorised guide to every episode of* Sex and the City. London: Virgin Books.

Smith, Neil. 2004. The channel that transformed TV. BBC News online, http://news.bbc.co.uk/2/hi/entertainment/3485916.stm (accessed March 14, 2007).

Sohn, Amy. 2004. *Sex and the City: Kiss and tell* (2nd ed., with revised text by Sarah Wildman). Basingstoke: Boxtree.

Stanley, Alessandra. 2003. Adieu, before the wrinkles show. *New York Times*, June 20, E1, 1.

Star, Darren. 2001. Interview for the Museum of Television and Radio

Seminar Series: Darren Star (MTR [NYC] recording ref T:67904 / 053672).

———. 2004. Interview for the Museum of Television and Radio Seminar Series: Primetime's hot addresses: The imagination of Darren Star (MTR [NYC] recording ref T:80657 / 060818).

Thompson, Robert J. 1997. *Television's second golden age: From* Hill Street Blues *to* ER. New York: Syracuse University Press.

Wilson, Elizabeth. (1991). *The sphinx in the city: Urban life, the control of disorder, and women*. London: Virgao.

Wolf, Naomi. 2003. Sex and the sisters. *Times* (London), July 20. http://www.timesonline.co.uk/tol/news/article845276.cce (accessed March 15, 2007).

Film

An Affair to Remember (Leo McCarey, 1957)
Annie Hall (Woody Allen, 1977)
Breakfast at Tiffany's (Blake Edwards, 1961)
The Devil Wears Prada (David Frankel, 2006)
Honeymoon in Vegas (Andrew Bergman, 1992)
If Lucy Fell (Eric Schaeffer, 1996)
L.A. Story (Mick Jackson, 1991)
Manhattan (Woody Allen, 1979)
Miami Rhapsody (David Frankel, 1995)
On the Town (Stanley Donen and Gene Kelly, 1949)
Sex and the City: The Movie (Michael Patrick King, 2008)
The Way We Were (Sydney Pollack, 1973)
The Wizard of Oz (Victor Fleming, 1939)

Television

Absolutely Fabulous (BBC, 1992–)
Beverly Hills 90210 (FOX, 1990–2000)
CSI: New York (CBS, 2004–)
Curb Your Enthusiasm (HBO, 2000–2005)
Designing Women (CBS, 1986–92)
Dynasty (ABC, 1981–89)
Friends (NBC, 1994–2004)
The Golden Girls (NBC, 1985–92)
Hart to Hart (ABC, 1979–84)
The Mary Tyler Moore Show (CBS, 1970–77)
Melrose Place (FOX, 1992–99)

Murphy Brown (CBS, 1988–98)
NYPD Blue (FOX, 1993–2005)
Rhoda (CBS, 1974–78)
Six Feet Under (HBO, 2001–5)
The Sopranos (HBO, 1999–2007)
That Girl (ABC, 1966–71)
Will and Grace (NBC, 1998–2006)